Essential Histories

The French Wars
1667–1714

The Sun King at war

Essential Histories

The French Wars 1667–1714

The Sun King at war

John A Lynn

First published in Great Britain in 2002 by Osprey Publishing,
Elms Court, Chapel Way, Botley, Oxford OX2 9LP, UK.
Email: info@ospreypublishing.com

ISBN 1 84176 361 6

Editor: Sally Rawlings
Design: Ken Vail Graphic Design, Cambridge, UK
Cartography by The Map Studio
Index by Bob Munro
Picture research by Image Select International
Origination by Grasmere Digital Imaging, Leeds, UK
Printed and bound in China by L. Rex Printing Company Ltd.

02 03 04 05 06   10 9 8 7 6 5 4 3 2 1

For a complete list of titles available from Osprey Publishing
please contact:

Osprey Direct UK, PO Box 140,
Wellingborough, Northants, NN8 2FA, UK.
Email: info@ospreydirect.co.uk

Osprey Direct USA, c/o MBI Publishing,
PO Box 1, 729 Prospect Ave,
Osceola, WI 54020, USA.
Email: info@ospreydirectusa.com

www.ospreypublishing.com

Contents

Introduction

The conflicts labeled as the wars of Louis XIV, which began in 1667 and concluded only in 1714, were very much the creations of that dazzling monarch. Louis, known to history as the Sun King because he adopted the sun as his emblem, conducted a luminous reign. French culture orbited about his magnificent presence, as he promoted art, architecture, literature, music, and

This famous portrait of Louis in state robes, painted by court painter Hyacinthe Rigaud in 1701, broadcasts the Sun King in all his glory as absolute monarch. (Ann Ronan Picture Library)

science. His grandeur reached far beyond culture, however, for he shone as king of the most powerful realm in Europe, with its richest economy and largest population, numbering 19–20 million souls by the close of the 17th century. In an age that knew violence all too well, it is no surprise that Louis asserted French preeminence by force of arms.

The wars of the Sun King engulfed western Europe, from Gibraltar to Germany, from Scotland to Sicily. Such extensive conflicts exerted a great influence on Europe. Borders changed permanently, and with them the fates of rulers, states, and peoples. Europe paid a huge price in blood and gold, as well. In straining the resources and capacities of governments, these struggles compelled states to develop institutions that

A brisk wind drives Dutch ships of the line across seas off the Netherlands during the Dutch War. (AKG, Berlin)

could tap and manage the riches necessary to succeed or simply survive. It is hard to imagine the development of 'absolutist' government without the pressures of war.

Armies and navies also took on new forms during this half-century of conflict. Basic outlines of the modern military emerged in France as Louis strove to enforce his claims on Europe through land campaigns. In addition, British naval dominance emerged from these struggles and with it the promise of colonial supremacy. The wars of the Sun King may not have produced the 'decisive' battles of Napoleon, but the style of warfare must be ultimately seen as valid and its impact on Europe as profound.

Chronology

1678 **1–9 March** French besiege and take Ghent
15–26 March French besiege and take Ypres
6 July Créqui wins battle of Rheinfeld
10 August First Treaty of Nijmegen ends war between France and the United Provinces
14 August Luxembourg defeats William at battle of St Denis
17 September Later Treaty of Nijmegen ends war between France and Spain; emperor signs on 6 February 1678

Era of the Reunions, 1679–84

1681 *Dragonnades* begin against Huguenots in Poitou
July–March 1682 French conduct first blockade of Luxembourg
30 September French seize Strasbourg

1683 **17 July–12 September** Turks besiege Vienna, but German and Polish forces relieve the city
31 August French declare they will send troops into Spanish Netherlands
26 October Spanish declare war on France; War of the Reunions begins

1684 **29 April–3 June** French besiege and finally take Luxembourg
17–28 May Duquesne bombards Genoa
15 August Truce of Ratisbon ends War of the Reunions

1685 **July** *Dragonnades* against Huguenots begin anew
22 October Louis revokes the Edict of Nantes with the Edict of Fontainebleau

1686 **April–June** Franco-Savoyard campaign attacks the Vaudois
July The League of Augsburg forms in Germany

Nine Years' War, 1688–97

1688 **24 September** Louis issues his 'Mémoire des raisons'
27 September–30 October Duras besieges and takes Philippsburg

5 November William lands in England to seize the crown
8–11 November French besiege and take Mannheim
26 November Dutch Republic enters war against France
December–June 1689 French devastate the Palatinate

1689 **March** James II sails to Ireland
11 May Château-Renault wins battle of Bantry Bay
12 May Grand Alliance formed between William and Leopold I
17 July–8 September German forces besiege and take Mainz
16 September–10 October German forces besiege and take Bonn

1690 **1 July** Luxembourg achieves his greatest tactical victory at battle of Fleurus
10 July Tourville defeats an Anglo-Dutch fleet at battle of Beachy Head
11 July William defeats James II at battle of the Boyne
18 August Catinat defeats Victor Amadeus at battle of Staffarde

1691 **15 March–10 April** Louis XIV besieges and takes Mons
24 March–2 April Catinat besieges and takes Nice
16 July Louvois dies
1 September–13 October Forces of William III besiege and take Limerick
19 September Luxembourg wins engagement at Leuze

1692 **29 May–3 June** Allied fleet defeats Tourville at battle of Barfleur– La Hogue
25 May–1 July French besiege and take Namur
3 August Luxembourg and William fight inconclusive battle of Steenkerque

1693 **21–22 May** De Lorge takes Heidelberg
1–13 June Noailles besieges and takes Rosas
27 June Tourville wins battle of Lagos
29 July Luxembourg defeats William III at battle of Neerwinden

10 September–10 October French besiege and take Charleroi
4 October Catinat wins battle of Marsaglia
1693–94 Famine strikes Continent
1694 **27 May** Noailles defeats Spanish at battle of the Ter
29 May–10 June French land and naval forces besiege and take Palamos
17 June–29 June Noailles besieges and takes Gerona
18 June Vauban repels Allied landing at Camaret near Brest
9 August Allied fleet arrives at Barcelona, forestalling French siege
17–27 September Allied army besieges and takes Huy
1695 **25 June–9 July** Savoyard forces take Casale in staged siege
1 July–6 September Allies besiege and take Namur
1696 **29 August** Treaty of Turin ends war between France and Duke of Savoy
1697 **15 May–5 June** French besiege and take Ath
12 June–10 August Vendôme and d'Estrées besiege and take Barcelona
8–27 September Baden besieges and takes Ebernberg
20 September Treaty of Ryswick ends war between France, United Provinces, England, and Spain
30 October Emperor signs Treaty of Ryswick
1698 **11 October** France, England, United Provinces, and the emperor sign partition treaty: Spain to go to Joseph Ferdinand
1699 **6 February** Joseph Ferdinand dies
1700 **25 March** France, England, and United Provinces sign another partition treaty
1 November Carlos II dies

War of the Spanish Succession, 1701–14

1701 **9 July** Eugene defeats Tessé at battle of Carpi

1 September Eugene defeats Villeroi at battle of Chiari
7 September Treaty of the second Grand Alliance between England, United Provinces, and Austria
1702 **1 February** Eugene attempts to seize Cremona; French hold it but Villeroi is captured
19 March William III dies
18 April–15 June Kaiserwerth falls to Allies
15 May England, the United Provinces, and Austria declare war against France
18 June–9 September Baden takes Landau
24 July Camisard uprising begins
August–September Anglo-Dutch fleet fails to take Cadiz
25 September Venlo capitulates to Allies
7 October Roermond capitulates to Allies
14 October Villars wins battle of Friedelingen
13–23 October Marlborough and Coehoorn besiege and take Liège
1703 **24 April–15 May** Marlborough takes Bonn
15–26 August Anglo-Dutch army besieges and takes Huy
15 August–6 September Tallard besieges and takes Breisach
20 September Elector of Bavaria and Villars win battle of Höchstädt
3 October Duke of Savoy declares war on France
12 October–17 November Tallard besieges and takes Landau
15 November Tallard defeats relief army at battle of Speyer
1704 **2 July** Marlborough defeats d'Arco at battle of Donauwörth
3 August Gibraltar capitulates to Anglo-Dutch force
13 August Marlborough and Eugene win battle of Blenheim
24 August French and Anglo-Dutch fleets face off in inconclusive battle of Velez-Málaga

1 October Villars proclaims pacification of Camisards

7 November Treaty of Ilbersheim ends fighting in Bavaria

1705   **5 May** Leopold I dies

16 August Vendôme wins battle of Cassano

22 August–9 October Allied forces take Barcelona

4–17 October Allies besiege Badajoz unsuccessfully

1706   **19 April** Vendôme wins battle of Calcinato

23 May Marlborough wins battle of Ramillies

26 May Brussels capitulates to Marlborough's army

30 May Ghent capitulates to Allies

6 June Antwerp capitulates to Allies

27 June Allies enter Madrid

9–18 August Allies take Menin

27 August–5 September Allies besiege and take Dendermonde

7 September Eugene wins battle of Turin

4 October Philip V returns to Madrid

1707   **3 March** Convention of Milan neutralizes Italy

25 April Berwick wins battle of Almanza

22–23 May Villars crosses the Lines of Stollhofen

28 July–22 August Allies unsuccessfully besiege Toulon

1708   **11 July** Marlborough and Eugene win battle of Oudenarde

14 August–8 December Marlborough and Eugene take Lille

1709 Famine strikes Continent

27 June–3 September Marlborough takes Tournai

11 September Marlborough and Eugene win costly battle of Malplaquet

1710   **9 March–20 July** Gertruydenberg Conference meets

27 July Staremberg wins battle of Almenara

20 August Staremberg wins battle of Saragossa

21 September Allies occupy Madrid again

3 December Philip V re-enters Madrid

9 December Vendôme wins battle of Brihuega

10 December Vendôme wins battle of Villa Viciosa

1711   **17 April** Joseph I dies, making Charles emperor

4–5 August Marlborough crosses French Ne Plus Ultra lines

11 August–12 September Marlborough takes Bouchain

8 October English and French conclude the 'London Preliminaries'

1712   **29 January** Utrecht Congress opens

May Queen Anne issues 'Restraining Orders'

24 July Villars defeats Eugene at Denain

30 July Marchiennes capitulates to Villars

31 July–8 September Villars takes Douai

21 August Suspension of arms between France, Great Britain, and Spain ends fighting in Spain

8 September–4 October Villars takes Le Quesnoy

7 November Suspension of arms ends fighting between France and Portugal

1713   **14 March** Suspension of arms ends fighting between France and Savoy

11–12 April Treaties of Utrecht end war between France, England, United Provinces, Savoy, Portugal, and Brandenburg-Prussia

11 June–19 August Villars takes Landau

22 September–16 November Villars takes Freiburg

1714   **7 March** Treaty of Rastatt ends war between Louis XIV and Charles VI

27 September Treaty of Baden ends war between France and Holy Roman Empire

7 July–12 September Philip V besieges and takes Barcelona

1715   **14–30 June** Franco-Spanish expedition takes Minorca

1 September Louis XIV dies

Themes of Louis's international policy

The Sun King naturally embraced warfare as a means of international policy, but that is hardly a surprising attitude for a monarch of his day. Louis lived his entire life immersed in war. He came to the French throne as a boy-king in the midst of the Thirty Years' War, which France had entered outright in 1635. When Louis XIII (r. 1610–43) died, his son had not reached the age of five, and as a child, Louis XIV could not actually rule. His mother, the Spanish-born queen, Anne of Austria, acted as regent, directed by Cardinal Mazarin, the extremely able first minister who had succeeded the consummate Cardinal Richelieu in 1642.

Although the Thirty Years' War ended in Germany with the Treaties of Westphalia in 1648, France enjoyed no respite because fighting continued with its arch-rival, Spain, for another 11 years. France had, in fact, been dueling with Habsburg Spain since the early 1500s. Spain experienced its greatest age during the 16th and early 17th centuries. The French monarchy saw itself surrounded by a chain of Spanish holdings, which included not only Spain itself, but the Spanish Netherlands (roughly today's Belgium) and the free county of Burgundy (Franche-Comté), linked by other lands clearly in the camp of the Spanish Habsburgs, such as Rhine bishoprics and the duchy of Lorraine. Cardinal Richelieu considered breaking this Habsburg encirclement and asserting French power as his primary goal, and he bequeathed this policy to Mazarin. By 1648 Spain was in decline, but the struggle with France had yet to be resolved.

Just at this point, a serious rebellion, the Fronde (1648–53), challenged the Bourbon monarchy. This revolt passed through several phases, during which those who resisted or rebelled embraced different programs of opposition. It began as a rejection of changes in administration and taxes, and ended by defending the power of the major princes of France, notably the Great Condé. The Fronde overlapped with the Spanish war, with Spain aiding the rebels. When the monarchy finally succeeded in defeating the rebellion, the proud Condé, who believed himself mistreated by his royal cousin, crossed over to the Spanish side and led enemy troops. The Treaty of the Pyrenees finally ended fighting with Spain in 1659, and as a mark of French victory, Louis married the Spanish infanta, Marie Thérèse.

In 1661 Cardinal Mazarin died. He had been not only first minister but also teacher and surrogate father for the young Louis. Under Mazarin's direction, Louis had learned the business of government, and when the Cardinal breathed his last, Louis's apprenticeship was over. He declared that he would run things on his own now, that there would be no first minister. The true reign, the personal reign, of Louis XIV began in 1661 and, therefore, we date the wars of Louis XIV only from that point.

The conflicts that concern us here include two minor clashes, the War of Devolution (1667–68) and the War of the Reunions (1683–84), plus three great wars, the Dutch War (1672–78), the Nine Years' War (1688–97), and the War of the Spanish Succession (1701–14). Even though Louis may have thought that some of these struggles were forced upon him, and he did not technically initiate all the conflicts, nevertheless aggressive French military action brought on, or helped to precipitate each of them. But even in this case, Spain's declaration of war can be read simply as a reaction to French armed aggression. The wars of the Sun King were, indeed, Louis's wars, and certain common themes underlay his bellicose actions and policies.

Europe in 1661

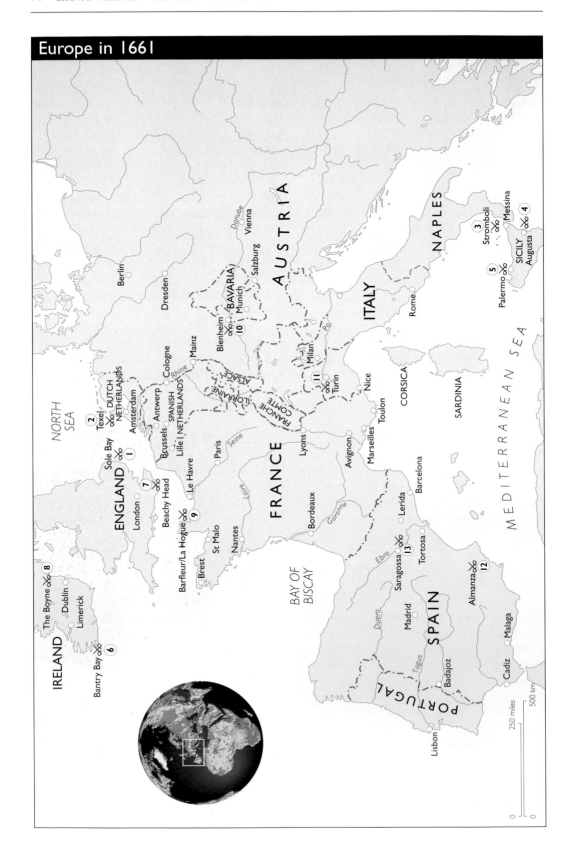

Louis's claims on the territory of Spain provided one important theme, not only because Spain was in decline, and thus ripe for the picking, but because its Habsburg dynasty was also faltering and the entire inheritance was almost certain to be contested. Two considerable figures ruled Spain during the 16th century: Carlos I (1519–56), who also ruled as Holy Roman Emperor Charles V, and his son, Philip II (1556–98), the autocratic, diligent, and profoundly religious monarch who launched the Armada against England. But Philip III (1598–1621) and Philip IV (1621–65) did not match their predecessors.

When Louis XIV, himself a grandson of Philip III, married the eldest surviving daughter of Philip IV, Marie-Thérèse, Louis garnered a strong claim to Spanish lands for his progeny. Marie-Thérèse abandoned all her rights to Spanish territory in her marriage contract, but this abrogation was contingent upon receipt of a very large dowry to be paid by the Spanish crown. Because this dowry was never paid, the French could later insist that she retained her rights. This gave Louis XIV and his dynasty a good claim to the vast holdings of Spain – a fact that would become important repeatedly during the rest of his life.

At the time of Louis's marriage to Marie, Philip IV was in his mid-fifties and it was not unreasonable to wonder what would happen at his death; in fact, Philip died in 1665. He was succeeded by his only son and heir, Carlos II (r. 1665–1700), a sickly and deformed child whom no one expected to survive long, although he outlasted all expectations. Louis immediately insisted that some Spanish lands were due to his wife, and at Carlos's death the Sun King accepted the entire inheritance for his grandson, precipitating the War of the Spanish Succession. Throughout Louis's personal reign, the cockpit of his wars was the Spanish Netherlands, and the lands he added to France consisted almost exclusively of Habsburg Spanish domains, including Franche-Comté and parts of Flanders, Artois, and Hainaut.

In an age that made a virtue of great pride, Louis pursued his *gloire*, (glory), with such concentration that it became an even more fundamental theme of French policy. Louis identified himself with the preeminence of France, and he would struggle to maintain and assert it. *Gloire* may be a word much out of fashion today, but defined as it ought to be, it is still a factor in

Vauban, Louis's great military engineer, was not only a builder and taker of fortresses but also a restless intellect who wrote on everything from pig breeding to the French tax system. (Ann Ronan Picture Library)

Parrocel's painting portrays Louis's army crossing the Rhine in 1672 at the start of the Dutch War. Louis always regarded this as one of the great triumphs of his reign. (Roger-Viollet)

personal and international relations. Above all, *gloire* meant reputation, and men of the 17th century regarded it as priceless. A king must establish his *gloire* through great accomplishments. As the practical Vauban insisted, 'True *gloire* does not flit like a butterfly; it is only acquired by real and solid actions.'

In the realm of foreign policy, Louis believed, 'Reputation is often more effective than the most powerful armies. All conquerors have gained more by reputation than by the sword.' There was a belligerent corollary for the young king: *gloire* could not be won without war, for it was essential to the very concept of kingship. In order to demonstrate his right to the throne, Louis must prove himself warrior and conqueror.

The pursuit of his *gloire* drove Louis's foreign policy; early in his reign he defined *gloire* in aggressive terms, while later he saw it as more defensive, as depending more on his capacity to protect than to expand his domains. When Mazarin disappeared from the stage, and Louis stepped out from behind the Cardinal's shadow, the young King Louis needed to define himself to his people and to Europe. It is not surprising that he sought conquests at the expense of the long-dynastic rivals of the French ruling family, the Habsburgs. Following a century and a half of French frustration before the power of the Habsburgs, Louis XIV now enjoyed the upper hand and squared off against the Spanish and eventually, their Australian cousins.

Given French strength and Louis's sense of his own grandeur, it was all but inevitable that he would pick a fight in Europe. John de Witt, the notable Dutch statesman, wrote in 1664 that France had:

a twenty-six year-old king, vigorous of body and spirit, who knows his mind and who acts on his own authority, who possesses a kingdom *populated by an extremely bellicose people and with very considerable wealth. Such a monarch would have to exhibit an extraordinary and almost miraculous moderation, if he stripped himself of the ambition which is so natural to all princes ... to extend his frontiers.*

   Once he had achieved significant conquests in the Dutch War and was proclaimed 'Louis the Great,' his *gloire* was assured, and his focus turned more to protecting his domains than to increasing them. The Sun King obsessed about constructing an impermeable barrier around his territory. In order to rationalize his borders into a stronger defensive line, however, he engaged in a series of limited seizures, the Reunions, which brought him such prizes as Strasbourg and Luxembourg.

To his mind these gains were steps toward a defensive goal, but his neighbors regarded them as further evidence of his insatiable lust for conquest.

The Nine Years' War came because he demanded that his neighbors recognize his rights to his new frontiers and because he wanted to close off one final route across the Rhine that left Alsace vulnerable. This conflict, his most critical miscalculation, resulted from a desire for defense that almost reached paranoia and an arrogance that tempted him to believe that he could bully Europe with impunity.

Louis ruled a France so mighty that it could, if need be, fight all its enemies single-handed. Louis sought allies to be sure, but he eventually alienated most of his neighbors and faced major alliances during his three great wars. It required powerful coalitions to oppose him.

The Sun King fought his wars in a distinct and separate orbit from conflicts to the east. These latter clashes at times affected some of the same parties involved in Louis's wars – Sweden, Brandenburg–Prussia, and Habsburg Austria – but the very different battles in northern Europe, eastern Europe, the Balkans, and Russia did not consume Louis's attention. To be sure, he tried to use such fights to his own advantage, aiding the Ottomans and Hungarian rebels in order to distract the emperor, for example. But his real efforts always centered on his own frontiers, where his policies promised direct gains for France and the Bourbon dynasty.

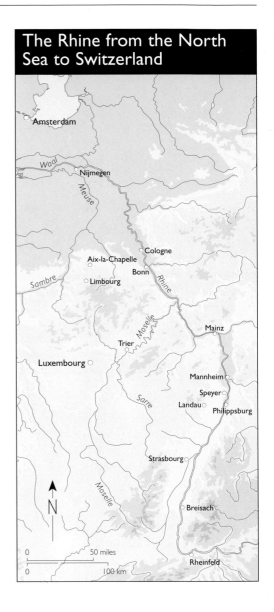

The Rhine from the North Sea to Switzerland

States, armies, navies, and warfare

An understanding of the wars of the Sun King must include the histories and policies of contending states and the power and limitations of contemporary armed forces. These were the parameters within which the narrative of the age unfolded. Having already considered the immediate past and goals of Louis's France, it is important to survey his enemies and allies.

Within this assemblage of states, continental interests contrasted with maritime focuses, dynastic goals with state needs. Perceived irreconcilability and a ready willingness to pursue political goals through violent means translated into warfare. The institutions and practices of armies and navies that fought the resultant conflicts were surprisingly similar, although military forces differed in size and resources. This was a time of important transitions, which some have called a Military Revolution, but European forces were advancing in the same direction. The interplay of states and forces produced a style of warfare best captured in the term 'war-as-process.' This describes not so much a goal as a result – a form of conflict in which the inability to achieve decision on the battlefield produced long wars of attrition.

Enemies and allies

Many European states became embroiled in the wars of Louis XIV, but time and space limit mention in this section to only six: Spain, the Dutch Republic, England, Habsburg Austria, Savoy, and Bavaria. At one point or another each would oppose Louis, yet all but the Austrian Habsburgs were also allied with France at some point.

Spain, already discussed as the erstwhile nemesis of France, became an object of desire, eventually gained by the Bourbons. At first Louis grabbed at Spanish lands on his northern and eastern borders. His armies generally campaigned against the Spanish in two areas, the Spanish Netherlands and Catalonia, although the Dutch War also brought fighting in Sicily. Bourbon claims on the Spanish Netherlands ran headlong into not only Spanish opposition, but also the commitment of the Dutch and, eventually, the English. The array of such formidable opponents on a vulnerable French frontier explains why Louis dispatched his largest armies to this front. Catalonia presented the possibility of carrying the war to Spain. Louis had reason to doubt Catalonian loyalty to their Habsburg king because this province had revolted against Philip IV from 1640 to 1652. During the Dutch War and the Nine Years' War, Louis committed small armies to play the Catalonian card.

The picture changed dramatically during the War of the Spanish Succession, when Spain, now a Bourbon monarchy, fought as an ally of France. In fact, Spain proved to be a burden for France because Louis now had to dispatch his troops and generals to campaign in the interior of Spain, from the Portuguese border to Barcelona. While ascending the Spanish throne marked a triumph for the Bourbon dynasty, it provided little benefit to the French state.

Before Louis's personal reign, the Dutch had stood with the French in opposing Spain for nearly a century. In response to growing demands by Philip II, the Netherlands, north and south, broke into rebellion in 1568. Philip struggled to reassert control over these rich provinces. The geography of the Netherlands determined that Spain, with the strongest armies of the 16th century, could dominate the south, but the north could shelter behind the river network at the mouth of the Rhine. The Spanish fought the Dutch Netherlands, formally known as the United Provinces, until 1648, so the Dutch speak of their Eighty Years' War. During this contest, the United Provinces emerged as independent, republican, Protestant, and immensely wealthy. Maritime commerce thrived as the Dutch developed the largest commercial fleet in Europe.

Through the generations-long fight against Spain, the Dutch shared common cause with the French. When he came to power, Louis assumed this natural affiliation would

Here the Duke of Marlborough, the finest English general of his age, perhaps of all ages, and nemesis of Louis during the War of the Spanish Succession wears the ceremonial armor typical of the portraits but obsolete in battle. (AKG, Berlin)

continue. He concluded a defensive alliance with the Dutch and lived up to its terms by supporting them with troops when the bishop of Münster occupied Dutch territory in 1665–66. Louis expected the Dutch to repay France by standing aside as he sought aggrandizement at the cost of Spain in the War of Devolution; instead, the Dutch blocked him. In retaliation, Louis attacked the United Provinces at the start of the Dutch War.

The Dutch now girded themselves for a series of clashes with Louis. The native princely house of Orange provided them with a leader, William III. While the United Provinces remained a republic, William III (1641–1702) emerged as its war leader, becoming stadholder and captain general for life, in 1672. With William's death in 1702, effective leadership of the United Provinces passed to the Grand Pensionary of Holland, Anthonie Heinsius (b. 1641, pensionary 1689–1720), who worked extremely well with the great English commander John Churchill (1650–1722), elevated in 1702 to the title of Duke of Marlborough.

At sea the Dutch possessed a hard-fighting fleet led by the great admiral Michiel de Ruyter (1607–76), who battled against the English and the French until his death late in the Dutch War. During the next great struggle, William III not only led the Dutch but also occupied the throne of England, and the Dutch fleet served alongside the increasingly predominant English Royal Navy.

Although the United Provinces is usually remembered as a naval power in the 17th century, it also fielded a small but impressive army. Some argue that regiment for regiment it was the toughest army in Europe. What few historians have realized to this point is the degree to which Dutch administrative talent and effort fed and supplied the large Allied armies in the Spanish Netherlands. Even Marlborough, who complained about the Dutch, could not have kept the field without them. The need to fight on land eventually lost the Dutch their naval competition with the English because the Dutch had to split their resources, while the English could invest above all in the navy and leave the creation of large armies to others.

William III lands with his Dutch troops at Torbay in November 1688 to claim the English throne. (Ann Ronan Picture Library)

After accepting the will of Carlos II, the aging Louis summons the court to recognize his grandson, the duc d'Anjou, as King Philip V of Spain. (Ann Ronan Picture Library)

The United Provinces eventually sought to protect its land by establishing a line of Dutch-garrisoned barrier fortresses on Spanish territory to hold off any potential French attack. Louis's seizure of these forts in the name of his grandson, who had become king of Spain, helped precipitate war in 1701.

Before 1689, England had been a sometime ally of the Bourbons, but after that date, it became a committed enemy. Spain had been a threat to England since the 16th century, and the English had collided with the Dutch in two wars, 1652–54 and 1665–67, although England had combined with the United Provinces to stop France in the Triple Alliance. If history provided some logic to an agreement between Charles II (b. 1630, r. 1660–85) and his first cousin, Louis XIV, Charles had new reasons of his own to drift into the orbit of the Sun King. The restored Stuart monarch wanted to reduce his financial dependence upon Parliament, and Louis allowed him to do so. In the secret Treaty of Dover (1670), Louis promised Charles a subsidy of 2,000,000 *livres* and 6,000 troops to put down any civil disturbance in England, and he could expect further subsidies if he joined in war against the Dutch. In return, Charles promised to declare himself Catholic when expedient and to break with the Dutch. The English fleet and some English regiments aided the French assault on the United Provinces in 1672, but this pro-French policy would not last long, as Parliament compelled Charles to pull out of the war in 1674. At the end of the Dutch War, the English threatened to re-enter the fighting, but now as an ally of the Dutch.

Louis misplayed his hand during the Glorious Revolution that unseated Charles's successor, James II (b. 1633, r. 1685–88). Concerned with a futile attempt to force the emperor into accepting French gains in the Reunions in perpetuity. Louis's force were concentrated in the Upper Rhineland and were unable to oppose the bold move by William III to take the English throne. William reigned as king 1689–1702 in tandem with his wife Mary (b. 1662, r. 1689–94). This Dutchman, the most inveterate foe of Louis XIV, brought England into alliances against the Sun King in the Nine Years' War and at the onset of the War of the Spanish Succession. His death did not bring down his work; Parliament and Queen Anne (b. 1665, r. 1702–14) continued the war policy.

England, which became 'Great Britain' after the 1707 union with Scotland, surpassed the Dutch and the French at sea and would continue to increase its advantage. Yet the British would not reap the full colonial rewards of their naval and maritime supremacy until the 18th century. During the personal reign of Louis, new English colonies dotted the coast of North America, and the British gained Acadia, Hudson Bay, and Newfoundland by the Treaty of Utrecht in 1713, but the Saint Lawrence valley remained French. At the opposite corner of the globe, the Moguls beat back attempts by the East India Company to take holdings in Bengal.

While the navy was ultimately to be the armed means to English wealth and power, the army nonetheless enjoyed its greatest moment of triumph during the last of Louis's great wars. William had been a first-rate diplomat and a good campaigner, but he was not the match of his French opponents, particularly Marshal Luxembourg. With William's passing, however, the English awarded command to their most superb general in history, the Duke of Marlborough. It is said of him that he never lost a battle or failed to take a fortress he besieged. While he receives praise for being a battle general in an age of sieges, it is worth noting that he fought only four or five great battles and conducted over 30 sieges.

If the maritime powers shared much in common, the Austrian Habsburgs stood in sharp contrast. The greatest honor possessed by the Austrian Habsburgs was their position as emperors of the Holy Roman Empire, a title awarded through election by a handful of the greatest princes of the empire, rulers known for this reason as electors. Leopold I occupied the imperial throne from 1658

Charles II (1630–85). Proclaimed king 1660. (Ann Ronan Picture Library)

until his death in 1705 when he was succeeded by his son Joseph I (b. 1678, r. 1705–11), who was followed by his brother Charles VI (b. 1685, r. 1711–40). But for all its honor and history, the Empire was not a state in the modern sense of the word, but rather an assemblage primarily of German principalities, along with German free cities, Bohemia lands, and holdings in northern Italy. The Reformation had shattered the Empire's religious unity, and the Thirty Years' War and the Treaties of Westphalia had left the Austrian Habsburgs reduced as emperors and exhausted as territorial rulers.

When he first assumed power, Louis could disregard the Habsburgs as weak, but they enjoyed a major resurgence during the last two decades of the 17th century, as they triumphed against the Ottoman Turks. For some time the true power base of the Habsburgs had been the domains they ruled personally; now these increased dramatically. The great campaign that climaxed in the Ottoman siege of Vienna in 1683 may have

ABOVE Sometimes forgotten by historians, Marshal Luxembourg was one of Louis's greatest commanders. Born a hunchback he did not let this physical handicap hold him back. (AKG, Berlin)

RIGHT The royal entourage on the road during wartime, Louis often brought members of the court, including his mistresses, to the front for spring campaigns. They traveled in grand style. (AKG, Berlin)

seemed to demonstrate a new surge of power for the Turks, but in fact it was a high water mark, and when the siege failed the waters receded far and fast. A string of victories, including Mohacs (1687) and Zenta (1697), gained Hungary, Transylvania, Croatia, and Slovenia for the Habsburgs.

Habsburg success to the east and south made the territories they ruled even more polyglot than before. The power of nationalism in the 19th century would doom Austria, but in the 17th century the main problem arising from the fact that the Habsburgs ruled over a mix of peoples was the welter of institutions and traditions that complicated and limited Habsburg authority. Yet however diverse their expanded territories, the Austrian Habsburgs could now draw on a greater resource base and so assert themselves more on the international stage. Understandably, Louis came to fear Leopold I as capable of upsetting the consolidation of his German border.

The relative rise of the Habsburgs made them a formidable adversary in alliance with

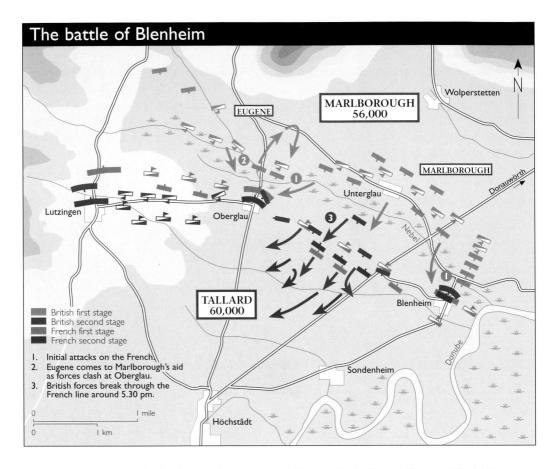

The battle of Blenheim

MARLBOROUGH
56,000

EUGENE

Wolperstetten

MARLBOROUGH

Donauworth

Lutzingen

Oberglau

Unterglau

Nebel

British first stage
British second stage
French first stage
French second stage

1.   Initial attacks on the French.
2.   Eugene comes to Marlborough's aid
     as forces clash at Oberglau.
3.   British forces break through the
     French line around 5.30 pm.

TALLARD
60,000

Blenheim

Sondenheim

Danube

0   1 mile
0   1 km

Höchstädt

the maritime powers. And whereas the Dutch always, and the English nearly always, restricted their continental deployment of troops to the Netherlands, Austrian Habsburg armies fought in Italy, the Rhineland, and the Spanish Netherlands. Imperial armies benefited from being commanded by two outstanding military figures, Raimondo Montecuccoli (1609–80) and Prince Eugene of Savoy (1663–1736). Prince Eugene rates as the finest general who ever served Austria. Paradoxically, he grew up in the French court, but Louis disliked the young Eugene, so he sought his fortune in Habsburg service. After his apprenticeship, he commanded the Emperor's armies against Louis in the War of the Spanish Succession.

It was not only great powers who engaged in the wars of the Sun King; second and third echelon states played roles as well. Lesser German states engaged in varying gambits during the wars of the Sun King. The Bavarian

Elector Maximilian II Emanuel (b. 1662, r. 1679–1726) stood by the Austrian Habsburgs during the Nine Years' War, but joined the French in the War of the Spanish Succession. His presence as a French ally explains the campaigns along the Danube 1703–04, which climaxed in the great triumph of Marlborough and Eugene at the battle of Blenheim. This victory cleared the Danube of French troops and left Bavaria occupied by the Habsburgs. Driven from his own lands, Maximilian Emanuel served, with some of his troops, in command of French armies in the Spanish Netherlands and along the Rhine. Louis honored his sacrifices and looked out for the interests of this Bavarian ally in the Treaty of Rastatt, which restored his lands and dignities.

Prince Eugene of Savoy, the greatest of Habsburg commanders, grew up around the French court, but the shame of his scandalous mother turned Louis against him, and he pursued his service in Imperial forces. (AKG, Berlin)

In Italy the most important belligerent was Savoy, which lay on the French border. Its duke, Victor Amadeus II (b. 1666, r. 1675–1730) would switch sides more than once. He sat out the Dutch War, but was bullied by Louis XIV in the 1680s and joined the anti-French alliance in 1690 during the Nine Years' War. When Savoy abandoned that alliance and concluded a settlement with the French in 1696, his act precipitated the end of the war. In spite of achieving several of the House of Savoy's key historical goals, he was developing a reputation for opportunistic duplicity which he increased by his conduct in the War of the Spanish Succession. Beginning the war in the French camp, he switched to the Grand Alliance in 1703. At first he suffered for this decision, as the French overran Savoy the next year, but a brilliant campaign by Eugene in 1706 forced the French to abandon Italy for good, much as Blenheim had driven Louis out of the Danube valley. Victor Amadeus's ambitions would be rewarded in the Treaty of Utrecht with the island of Sicily and a royal title.

Armies, the French paradigm

The military development of France under Louis XIV became a model for Europe, encouraging like organization, administration, and tactics. The Sun King boasted the largest army of his day, and the most indomitable battalions on the Continent, at least until they were humbled in the War of the Spanish Succession.

Considering the long run of history, perhaps the most important aspect of the wars of the Sun King was their increased scale, and nothing demonstrates this more than the dramatic growth in the size of armies. The French royal army expanded rapidly during the 17th century. From the late Middle Ages through the early 1600s, wartime strength usually peaked at no more than 60,000–70,000 men, and such numbers were maintained only for weeks before returning to lower levels. Between conflicts,

the monarchy rarely maintained in excess of 10,000 men. Traditionally, we have estimated that the peak number of troops mobilized during the Richelieu at 125,000, but recent careful research suggests that this must be lowered to 70–80,000 in the field, plus garrison forces. Garrisons would raise the numbers, but not to 125,000. In any case, it is difficult to know the size of the army during the Thirty Years' War with any certainty. Following the Treaties of Westphalia, the army shrank, even though France remained at war with Spain.

The Sun King raised army size to unprecedented heights, as shown by official, or paper, figures: 134,000 during the War of Devolution, 279,000 during the Dutch War, 440,000 during the Nine Years' War, and 377,000 for the War of the Spanish Succession. By carefully comparing paper figures with select muster figures of real units on campaign, it is possible to discount these numbers to estimate how many men were literally present under arms. Such a method suggests that the real wartime strength of Louis's army hit a maximum of a bit over 350,000 during the Nine Years' War. At the same time, Louis constantly increased the proportions of his peacetime, or standing, army. After the Dutch War, the number of troops kept in service between wars reached about 150,000, a 15-fold multiplication of the peacetime levels existing at the start of the 17th century.

Louis's army represented a new pattern of military force. The troops of Louis XIV were no longer composed largely of mercenary bands and private forces supplied by powerful nobles, as had been the armies of his forebears. Cumulative reforms dating back to Richelieu and Louis XIII, but accelerated by Michel LeTellier, war minister under Mazarin and then Louis XIV, and the Marquis de Louvois, LeTellier's son and successor, set the pattern. Instead of relying on hired bands, this new style of army was composed of royal regiments, laboriously raised, supplied, and trained. They were directly responsible to, and obedient to, the king. The structure and size of units from companies to brigades, along with the hierarchies of the officers within them, became very much what they are today. The battalion of 500–800 troops constituted the fundamental French combat infantry unit; one or more battalions formed a regiment. Cavalry formed in squadrons of about 140 during the War of the Spanish Succession, and two or three squadrons made up a regiment.

This force relied primarily upon voluntary enlistment to fill the ranks, although one form of limited conscription or another could top up manpower requirements. Recruits were supposed to present themselves for service willingly. Recruiting parties tried to lure them with marshal display and tempt

An engraving by Hainzelman c. the mid-1680s. Louvois, the imperious war minister of Louis XIV, reached the zenith of his powers in the 1680s, as he appears in this engraving by Hainzelman. Louvois's ample flesh belies his hard-handed and brutal policies. (AKG, Berlin)

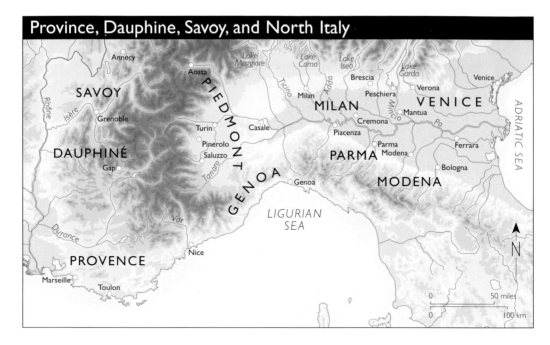

Province, Dauphine, Savoy, and North Italy

them with recruitment bounties, which varied according to supply and demand. French regiments made up the bulk of Louis's army, but he also mustered foreign regiments, which were structured with the same regularity and subjected to the same obedience as native units.

The state asserted its control over its armed forces as never before. Previous to the personal reign of Louis XIV, generals often operated as if they were independent princes. However, the Sun King imposed greater order on his generals, particularly after Turenne's death; seniority became the principle for precedence among high-level commanders, and obedience was expected and enforced at all levels.

Changes in administration and command accompanied this transformation of army size, composition, and control. To manage these larger, more regular, and more expensive armies, governments created or vastly expanded the military ministries. LeTellier and Louvois multiplied their staffs and their workload. Through elaborate and costly logistical arrangements, the government fed its troops instead of letting them fend for themselves and royal inspectors strived to ensure proper clothing

and equipment for the troops. It is highly illustrative that uniforms became standard at this time. Convoys snaked from grain magazines, to field ovens, to camps, providing the necessary bread. Government-purchased herds supplied meat. As much as possible, French military administration strove to take care of the troops because authorities feared that ill-clothed and starving soldiers would desert, or at least turn to marauding and thus dissolve discipline and unit integrity.

Despite all the efforts of the state, the expenses of these huge armies often exceeded available funds; therefore, all antagonists tried to commandeer local resources. Troops drew on local forage for horses by dispatching war parties to harvest it in nearby fields. And, of the utmost importance, armies imposed war taxes, or 'contributions,' to be paid in kind or in money by unfortunate villages and towns in the war zone. The need to collect contributions sometimes became a determinant of strategy.

As to weapons and tactics, French infantry still carried matchlock-muskets and pikes early in Louis's personal reign, to be exchanged for flintlock fusils and bayonets

after 1700. Other armies, including the English and Dutch, made this transition a bit earlier. Both musket and fusil were reasonably effective at 50–100 yds (45–90 m) against large formations, but neither smoothbore was a sharpshooter's weapon. Limitations in range and accuracy doomed infantry to blasting away at close quarters,

Court painter Pierre Mignard shows Louvois, the imperious war minister of Louis XIV, as he was at the peak of his power. He wears the robes of the Ordre de Saint Esprit. (Roger-Viollet)

with deadly results. Infantry tactics evolved slowly, but they were always based on a linear deployment of battalions. The old mass squares of the early 17th century had disappeared from the battlefield before Louis's personal reign. Cavalry shed more armor and relied primarily on the sword. Cannon hurled various packets of death across the field, with the big 24pdr siege cannon highly effective at 600 yds (550 m) and capable of inflicting casualties at 2,000 yds (1,830 m). Artillery began battles at long range, and combat often climaxed with pounding hooves and slashing swords, but infantry was the queen of battles.

Battle by nature was a theater of chance and risks, requiring high casualties to achieve doubtful outcomes; this reality made siege warfare all the more preferable. The science and art of fortress design reached its peak with the work of Sébastien le Prestre de Vauban, the great engineer who served Louis. He certainly did not originate this low-lying style of fortifications, but he carried it to a higher level of perfection. Engineers carefully plotted the angles of the arrowhead-shaped bastions so that cannon and musket fire from one could sweep the ditches in front of the others to each side. In this way the bastions functioned less as walls than as mutually supporting strong points with intersecting fields of fire. In 1673 Vauban transcended the design of individual fortresses to propose the Pré Carré, or dueling ground, which would provide a defense in depth composed of two lines of fortress across the northeast frontier of France.

Sieges against such fortresses were rational and predictable. Before the formal siege began, a fortress was surrounded, 'invested,' by cavalry. Next, commandeered peasants, or 'pioneers,' dug siege lines. Lines of circumvallation faced outward at a distance of a mile (1.6 km) or more all around the fortress to protect the besieging army from enemy relief forces. Lines of contravallation faced inward to contain the garrison and provide protection against sorties. Once well established, the besiegers opened approach trenches and drove them toward the fortress. Vauban's system of attack employed three 'parallels' – trenches dug parallel to the side of the fort chosen for the main attack. The

first parallel was situated 600 yds (550 m) from the fortress and mounted batteries to batter its walls.

Increasingly from the Dutch War through the War of the Spanish Succession, contending armies constructed long defensive field fortifications at times stretching over 100 miles (160 km). Such lines were originally intended only to stop enemy raiding parties and thus shelter friendly territory and protect resource bases; however, they became more substantial with time and, if occupied by a large number of troops, could stymie entire armies. These lines employed rivers, inundations, and other defensible terrain, if possible, and on open ground employed trench lines constructed with all the science and art of fortification.

Navies

For Louis, wars were contests over glory, territory, and sovereignty on the Continent, but they were fought at sea as well, and this turned to a great advantage for the English. Naval warfare was very much about the ships. That seems a truism, but it contains an essential and less obvious fact: preeminence at sea resulted from numbers of sailing ships, and this depended more on construction, and thus on a state's willingness to commit resources to the navy, than it did on the fate of battles. Certainly, in the Mediterranean, galleys could still be useful, but the real crux was the sailing fleet. England would win the naval war more in the shipyards than at sea.

The French navy boasted few ships under Richelieu and Mazarin, but Jean-Baptiste Colbert, Louis's naval minister, sharply expanded it. By 1672 the navy had 120 major vessels, at a time when Dutch numbers were declining, from 129 in 1670 to 93 a decade later. The French could handle a naval war with the United Provinces, but the alliance of the two maritime powers overwhelmed Louis. During the Nine Years' War, the French battle fleet numbered 119 vessels in 1695, while the combined English and Dutch fleets already counted 189. From 1694 to 1697, the French built 19 first- to fifth-rate ships, totaling 15,410 tons, while the English constructed 58 such vessels, totaling 41,844 tons and the Dutch added another 22. By 1700 the French navy had only 108 major ships to the English and Dutch count of 210.

To a surprising degree, fleet operations were linked with land campaigns in this period – naval power was by nature amphibious for all naval powers. For Louis, the greatest danger from the sea was not an assault on his commerce but a descent on his shores. At the same time, Louis conducted operations in Ireland and threatened other landings in the British Isles. Naval power was also essential to carry out coastal sieges. Attempts to take Barcelona always required command of the waters off that port, for example.

Ultimately the French suffered from multiple disadvantages in a naval contest with the English and the Dutch. Without as large a maritime commerce as benefited the Allies, the French were perpetually short of skilled sailors. Despite its extensive coastline, France lacked large deep-water ports to house a fleet. Only Brest on the Atlantic and Toulon on the Mediterranean sufficed. The very placement of the ports also posed a problem; they were too far from Paris, so it took too long for correspondence and orders to go back and forth. But above all these very real problems, the paramount and insurmountable obstacle to French naval preeminence was the monarchy's need to concentrate its resources on land rather than at sea.

Louis eventually made a very conscious decision to cast his navy adrift. During the Nine Years' War, as the army grew immensely, Louis determined that he could not increase both his army and his navy, and after 1695 he sacrificed the latter. Experience showed that the French could defend their coasts as effectively and far more cheaply with land forces. At this point, the French turned from fleet warfare, *guerre d'escadre*, to commerce raiding, *guerre de course*. Maintaining a much reduced royal navy, the French turned to privateers, who were privately financed commerce raiders carrying letters of marque that officially recognized them as fighting in the name of the king against designated enemies. The letter of marque distinguished a privateer from a pirate. As a rule, private investors bought and outfitted ships for privateering; however, in the French case, the king offered supplies and ammunition and would even lease royal navy vessels to privateers.

'War-as-process'

The style of warfare that typified the reign of the Sun King contrasted strongly with that practiced by Napoleon a century later. Louis's wars conformed to a pattern that can be termed 'war-as-process'. This had five characteristics: the indecisive character of battle and siege; the slow tempo of operations; the powerful influence of attrition; the need to make war feed war; and the considerable emphasis given to ongoing diplomatic negotiations. These qualities stand out in high relief when compared to what can be called Napoleonic 'war-as-event,' defined as: the decisive character of battle, an event; the rapid tempo of operations; the minimal influence of attrition and the consequent lack of pressure to make war feed war, because wars concluded rapidly; and the minimal role of diplomacy in ending war, since diplomats had only to recognize and legitimize the *fait accompli* established by force of arms.

In 'war-as-process', neither battle nor siege decided wars. The presence of numerous fortifications in a theater of war dampened the effect of defeat because a vanquished force could shelter behind stone walls to recoup and collect reinforcements. The fact that states geared up slowly for great wars meant that conflicts became grand, multi-front affairs before one side or the other could strike a knockout blow. Multi-front wars tended to stagnate because one front could supply reserves to buttress another, further dampening the effects of defeat. Hobbles on mobility, such as elaborate and slow supply arrangements, limited the ability to drive an

Jean Bart (1651–1702), who sailed from Dunkirk to raid English commerce, epitomizes the French tradition of privateers engaged in *guerre de course*. (Ann Ronan Picture Library)

enemy into a corner or pursue him. The fact that these armies could only campaign for about six or seven months a year also gave an army that had been set back on its heels the time it required to recover.

Attrition – that is, the high cost of war fought year after year – strained the resources of the belligerents and determined operational decisions. Louis would cancel plans for a siege, for example, simply because it was too costly. In this environment of attrition, where the mobilization of resources for war was critical, adversaries tried to make war feed war. Entire campaigns might be fought to milk enemy territory for everything it was worth rather than to achieve some grand strategic goal.

While war was fought by armies, it was also waged by diplomats. Diplomacy exerted such influence because there were three players at the table: the military course of the war, attrition, and negotiations. In the long run, attrition could negate success in the field, and diplomacy had to find a way out. Negotiators plied their trade year after year, often in the cold months between campaign seasons. Having able generals in command of the troops mattered greatly, of course, but so did having skillful diplomats at courts and conferences.

Drawing the sword

The several conflicts of the Sun King involved a constant repertoire of themes, a stock cast of characters, and a similar practice of war, but they were still very different dramas one from the other. Notably, the specific *casus belli* varied; there was no single reason for drawing the sword.

Louis justified his first war by insisting that his wife should inherit some territory when her father, Philip IV, died in 1665. Louis did not dispute the right of her half brother, Carlos II, to the throne and the vast majority of Spanish domains. However, Louis argued that custom in parts of the Spanish Netherlands held that the children of a man's first marriage, even daughters, had rights of inheritance superior to children of a second marriage. By an extension of this logic, Louis insisted that Marie-Thérèse should receive a portion of the Spanish Netherlands. Louis produced a document developing this case and circulated it in Europe, but beyond this, the pursuit of his own *gloire* seems to have been a critical motive. Still, he insisted that this War of Devolution was not a French invasion but an attempt of his queen to claim her rightful inheritance.

His forces crossed the border in May 1667 against minimal opposition. The most serious action of the campaign concerned the brief siege of Lille. Spain may not have mounted a serious opposition, but Louis's erstwhile friends, the United Provinces, England, and Sweden, did. Alarmed at Louis's acquisitions, these states formed the Triple Alliance in January 1668, declaring that Louis could keep what he had already conquered but that, should he continue to take more, the alliance would enter the war on the side of Spain. Unprepared for a long war against such formidable foes, Louis grudgingly made peace, receiving several new towns, most notably Lille, as his reward.

Louis's next conflict, the Dutch War, was very much a child of the first. Louis viewed the intervention of the Dutch in the War of Devolution as a betrayal. He charged them with 'ingratitude, bad faith, and insupportable vanity.' A medal struck in the United Provinces portrayed Joshua stopping the sun in its course; the reference to the Sun King was painfully obvious. Louis prepared now for a war to humble and neutralize the Dutch so as to clear the way for him to do as he pleased in the Spanish Netherlands. He showed more diplomatic finesse in preparing for the coming war than

Emperor Leopold I, shown below, led a rising Holy Roman Empire against the mighty France of the Sun King. (AKG, Berlin)

he displayed in any of his other conflicts. He detached Sweden from the Triple Alliance with money payments and signed the Treaty of Dover with Charles II. In November 1671 Louis concluded a treaty with Emperor Leopold I by which Leopold promised neutrality in case of a Franco–Dutch War, as long as the Treaties of Westphalia and the Peace of Aix-la-Chapelle were respected.

For Louis, attacking the Dutch might simply be a preamble to another invasion of the Spanish Netherlands, but he could not assault the Spanish directly because such aggression would trip defensive agreements with other states, bringing allies to the aid of Spain. Thus, Louis planned to avoid Spanish territory when advancing to the Dutch border by marching through the bishopric of Liége in April 1672. Louis hoped that his assault on the Dutch would provoke an overtly offensive response by Spain, which would void the obligation of its allies to fight at its side. With the Dutch pushed out of the way and Spain isolated, he would have his way in the Spanish Netherlands; but this was not to happen, as will be seen.

The War of the Reunions came as the result of Louis's seizures of towns, fortresses, and land designed to create defensible frontiers. Louis's statements about protecting his borders have often been dismissed as sheer casuistry designed to cover his naked aggression, but such a criticism does not recognize that the Sun King felt real anxiety. Even the level-headed Vauban counseled the need to add some of the important acquisitions to rationalize the frontier. The Spanish government understandably saw itself abused and threatened by the Reunions – so much so that Spain declared war on Louis in October 1683. Spain foolishly expected the Austrian Habsburgs to come to its aid, but they were concerned with repelling the Ottoman invasion. The Dutch supplied some troops, but there were not enough to hold back the French, who triumphed by August 1684.

The Nine Years' War, also known as the War of the League of Augsburg or the War of the Grand Alliance, stands out as Louis's

greatest blunder. The treaty that ended the War of the Reunions promised only a 20-year-long truce, not a permanent settlement. Louis continued his aggressive ways in Italy during the spring of 1686 by insisting that the Duke of Savoy forcibly convert his own Protestant Vaudois community, and then imposing French troops on him to do the job. Louis's bullying drove a number of German states, including Habsburg Austria, along with representatives of Sweden and Spain, to form the League of Augsburg in July 1686 to oppose further French aggression.

Louis, however, saw himself threatened and badly wanted a perpetual guarantee of his Reunions because he believed, with good reason, that the Austrian Habsburgs would turn on France once they had concluded their war with the Ottomans. In 1687 he demanded that the Habsburgs sanction his gains, but they refused. Louis also feared that the important archbishopric of Cologne, which sheltered part of his frontier, would go to an individual hostile to France when the current archbishop, Max Henry, gave up the ghost. Crisis struck in June 1688 when Max Henry died.

Louis hoped that one more short war would compel the Germans to concede the necessary assurances. As leverage and shield, Louis resolved to take the Rhine fortress of Philippsburg. His province of Alsace had suffered from Allied incursions during the Dutch War, and he wanted to close off the Rhine frontier to preserve it in the future. Of the Rhine crossings that threatened Alsace, Philippsburg was the last that remained outside his control. By seizing it, Louis would make a display of force that would protect Alsace and cower the Germans into accepting his terms. The Marquis de Louvois assured the Sun King that this would require only three or four months.

On 24 September 1688 Louis issued his 'Mémoire des raisons,' explaining his 'righteous' rationale for taking up arms once more, and a French army overwhelmed Philippsburg, which fell on 20 October. But instead of conceding to his wishes, the

Germans united against Louis. Major princes, including the Elector of Brandenburg and the Duke of Hanover quickly sent troops. Soon the emperor opposed Louis; in March 1689 the Dutch joined the fight, and in May, England entered the fight against Louis. European states leagued together because they read the attack across the Rhine simply as further evidence that only force would stop Louis. Compromise would be impossible with such a conqueror.

Louis's last war came despite his efforts to avoid conflict. The Nine Years' War proved so costly that a chastised Louis sought peace, at almost any price. It was clear that the childless Carlos II would not survive much longer on the Spanish throne, and the other great powers hoped to settle the distribution of the Spanish inheritance without embroiling Europe in another war.

Three candidates could claim the right to succeed Carlos. The Dauphin, son of Louis and Marie-Thérèse, held a particularly strong suit because both his grandmother and mother were Spanish princesses, and eldest daughters to boot. Spanish custom allowed succession to or through daughters in the absence of sons. Emperor Leopold I, a grandson of Philip III, just as was Louis XIV, put forward his second son, Archduke Charles, reserving the imperial title for his first son, Archduke Joseph. A dispute between the Dauphin and the Archduke would lead to war, but fortunately a third candidate promised a way to avoid conflict; Joseph Ferdinand, the son of elector Maximilian Emanuel of Bavaria, held a weaker but convenient claim. A partition treaty accepted by Louis XIV, Leopold I, and William III would award Spain, the Spanish Netherlands, and the colonies to the electoral prince, while the Dauphin would receive Naples, Sicily, and fortresses in Tuscany, with the Archduke getting Milan. Because the Dauphin was in line for the French throne, his gains would merge with France on his accession.

In a metaphor of the Nine Years' War, this engraving from an almanac of 1689 shows Louis fighting alone against the combined states of Europe. Louis has already vanquished heresy and ignorance, which lay at his feet. (Roger-Viollet)

Louis XIV in his prime, at about age 40, astride a white charger. In his painting, Houasse displays Louis's very real abilities as a talented and tireless horseman. (AKG, Berlin)

The death of Joseph Ferdinand early in 1699 scuttled this settlement, and once more Louis sought a peaceful accommodation. He and William agreed to award Archduke Charles all the inheritance earmarked for the electoral prince, while the Dauphin would receive a far more modest share composed of the earlier concessions meant for him plus Milan. However, Leopold would have nothing of it and refused to limit his son's claims.

None of these arrangements considered the wishes of Carlos II, who wanted above all that his domains remain intact. As he lay on his deathbed in 1700, Carlos, who judged the French best able to defend his domains, dictated a will that offered his entire inheritance to Philip of Anjou, the second son of the Dauphin. Carlos did not want Spain to unite with France, so he did not offer his crown to a French prince immediately in the line of succession; this ruled out the Dauphin and his eldest son. The will of Carlos II stipulated that if Philip of Anjou declined the inheritance, it would be offered to his younger brother, the Duke of Berry. However, if both French princes turned down the bequest, the rider would proceed to Vienna and promise everything to Archduke Charles.

Louis met with his ministers to weigh the options. To accept the partition treaty of 1699 would win peace with William, but Charles would still demand everything, requiring Louis to fight a war with the Emperor. In this case, the Emperor would have Spain as an ally, and the only spoils the Bourbons could hope for would be in Italy. However, if Louis accepted the will, he would have Spain as an ally and the entire inheritance could be secured for the Bourbon family, although no lands would go directly to France in the future. Not surprisingly, Louis opted to support the legitimate claims of his grandson.

This meant war with the emperor, as would have pursuit of the partition treaty, but it did not have to mean war against another Grand Alliance. However, Louis, guided once again by pride, acted in such an overweening way as to virtually guarantee the major war he so much wanted to avoid. Louis issued letters patent expressly maintaining Philip's right to ascend to the French throne, although his father, his elder brother, and any son his elder brother might have were ahead of Philip in the line of succession. Louis almost certainly saw this as recognizing God-established laws of royal inheritance, not as an attempt to unite the two crowns. Next, Louis infuriated William III by occupying the precious barrier fortresses with French troops to secure them for Philip.

As if threatening the Dutch were not enough, Louis went on to alienate the English. He secured the *asiento*, the right to supply slaves to the Spanish colonies, for French traders, when English commercial interests wanted it. Louis also insisted on recognizing the son of James II as the rightful king of England when the father died. Again, Louis's strong belief in divine right explains this, but it was certainly an inopportune time to make such a declaration. Once again Louis appeared to be a dangerous bully; William III responded by forming a new coalition to oppose him.

French cannon bore the inscription, 'Ultima Ratio Regis,' the final argument of the king. Louis resorted to this kind of argument too often. His first two wars were a product of aggression in pursuit of victory and aggrandizement that would establish his *gloire*. He sought those wars. His last two great conflicts grew beyond anything he had intended, but he did not do everything in his power to avoid or to limit them. Louis bears the responsibility for the onset of each of his wars, even if they did not turn out to be the kind of conflicts he had envisioned.

The campaigns for *gloire*

The Sun King's five wars arched the span of nearly 50 years. Louis would be one of the very few individuals who lasted the full odyssey; most fell by the wayside at some point during the trek, while others joined in down the road. The constant presence of Louis may give an impression of continuity that masks contrast and evolution. Without denying common elements that allow us to generalize about this era of conflict, no simple statements can fully encompass such a breadth of time and action. Only a narrative of the wars, their course from day to day, can reveal them.

The War of Devolution

Louis set his first war into motion by announcing his claim to land in the Spanish Netherlands early in May 1667 and then dispatching an army commanded by Turenne to seize it. Turenne began the campaign by taking Armentières. The Spanish could oppose Louis's forces with only a modest number of troops, and the French advance moved apace, as fortresses capitulated with only a few days' resistance; Tournai fell on 25 June, Douai on 6 July, and Courtrai on 18 July.

As so often was the case, Louis accompanied his army, a practice he continued until age caught up with him in 1693. On his visits to the front, he usually came with gentlemen and ladies of the court. In May 1667 he hosted his wife and two mistresses in the same coach. He first left them in Compiègne, but by July Louis called up his court entourage and so gave the conquered areas a view of their new queen. One contemporary commented on his train in 1667, 'All that you have seen of the magnificence of Solomon and the grandeur

of the king of Persia does not equal the pomp displayed on this trip.'

The French juggernaut encountered the most serious resistance at Lille. Louis attended while the French first constructed lines of circumvallation and contravallation, and then opened attack trenches on the night of 17–18 August. The Spanish commander capitulated on 27 August.

The French went into winter quarters early that fall, but the diplomats then began their work. The result was the Triple Alliance, which joined the United Provinces, England, and Sweden in a combination to frustrate Louis's desire for further conquests. Before concluding peace in May 1668, Louis put the Great Condé, finally returned to the King's good graces, in charge of an army that took Franche-Comté, although this would be returned to Spain in the subsequent Peace of Aix-la-Chapelle. This agreement rewarded France with Charleroi, Tournai, Courtrai, Ath, Furnes, Douai, some other portions of the Spanish Netherlands, and, above all, Lille.

The Dutch War

Short and cheap, the War of Devolution turned out to be an anomaly; the Dutch War, which grew out of the earlier conflict, far better exemplified the problems faced by Louis. Initial diplomatic success in isolating his foe dissolved, and he soon faced a powerful coalition on several fronts. While he finally reaped some important gains, he fell short of being able to dictate a settlement in the Spanish Netherlands.

Louis believed he had the war he wanted in 1672, one that would allow him to punish the Dutch and force them to grant him a free hand against Spain. After declaring war in April, the French advanced north through

Challenge at the Coronation of James II. (Ann Ronan Picture Library)

the archbishopric of Liège in two main armies commanded by Turenne and Condé, with a third under Luxembourg along the Rhine. At roughly 150,000 men in total, the French army was large, but not yet ponderous. LeTellier and Louvois had prepared for the advance by stockpiling the necessities of war, and this probably rates as Louis's best-managed campaign. Towns and fortresses capitulated as expected; Rheinberg, Wesel, Burick, and Orsoy fell in days. Condé's army crossed the Rhine on 12 June at Tolhuis, a feat Louis would later celebrate with a large metaphoric plaster relief in the Salle de Guerre at Versailles. The French took Deventer and moved on to seize Utrecht, where Louis made a ceremonial entry on 30 June; Nijmegen surrendered on 9 July.

In late June, the desperate Dutch offered generous peace terms, which included granting France Dutch-held lands in Brabant and Flanders, the fortress of Maastricht, and a large indemnity, but Louis haughtily declined. Even before Louis rejected the offer, the Dutch opened the sluices at Muiden, flooding the approaches to Amsterdam and thus protecting the city. This crucial action forestalled the French, who needed to take Amsterdam to break the Dutch.

The war soon expanded, as the elector of Brandenburg honored his commitment to the United Provinces. Turenne led an army to the Rhine, parried the elector's thrust, and drove him back across northern Germany, compelling him to exit the war. Meanwhile,

Emperor Leopold I entered the lists against Louis without formally declaring war at first. The emperor's general, Raimondo Montecuccoli, outmaneuvered Turenne and joined forces with the new Dutch stadtholder, William III, in November 1673.

Although 1673 failed to bring a decision in the United Provinces, the French took Maastricht that June. In order to maintain their momentum the French had bypassed that fortress in 1672, but now they retraced their steps. Defended by a garrison of 6,000 troops, Maastricht promised to be a difficult target. On 10 June, Louis joined the army of 45,000 that he had ordered to undertake the task. The French commandeered 7,000 peasants to dig the lines of circumvallation and contravallation,

which were finished on 14 June. Then sappers opened the attack trenches on the night of 17–18 June. Vauban, who directed the siege, first used his system of parallels here, and on 30 June the garrison asked for terms, surrendering the next day.

In 1674 the war shifted from the United Provinces to the Spanish Netherlands, or

ABOVE Marshal Turenne ranks as one of Louis's greatest commanders. Proud and demanding, Turenne continued to sharpen his skills as he aged until struck down by a cannonball in 1675. (Ann Ronan Picture Library)

RIGHT Here the Great Condé commands at his victorious battle of Lens (28 August 1648). Like Turenne, Condé served Louis XIII and Mazarin before leading troops in the wars of the Sun King. (Ann Ronan Picture Library)

'Flanders.' In military discussions, the French referred to the Spanish Netherlands from the Meuse valley west as 'Flanders,' although technically that was only one of the provinces in the area. We will follow that practice here. Goaded by Louis, the Spanish entered the war outright in October 1673. The elector of Brandenburg rejoined the contest, and the Holy Roman Empire declared war in May 1674. By this point, the English had abandoned their alliance with France. Faced with this new situation, Louis pulled his troops out of the Dutch Netherlands. The Great Condé commanded Louis's main army in Flanders, where the high point of his campaign saw him win a

particularly bloody but inconclusive victory against William at Seneffe on 11 August.

That year, Turenne fought a masterly, if brutal, campaign on the borders of Alsace. In quick moves, he advanced across the Rhine and won a largely cavalry action at Sinzheim on 16 June 1674. After returning to Alsace, Turenne broke across the Rhine once more to strike at Heidelberg, forcing the imperial army to retreat. Throughout much of the summer Turenne supplied, or 'subsisted,' his troops off the resources of the Palatinate, making war feed war. His army destroyed what it did not consume, and by denuding the area he protected Alsace from an imperial advance. When an enemy army approached, Turenne blocked it, and unable to subsist on the little the French had left in the Palatinate, the imperials retired in September.

The imperial general Bournonville was not without his own gambits, and he next seized the neutral city of Strasbourg and crossed its bridge into Alsace. Learning that the elector of Brandenburg was marching to join Bournonville, Turenne attacked Bournonville at Ensheim on 4 October. French victory there forced Bournonville to retire, but Turenne could not stop him from linking up with the elector. At this point Turenne pulled back in the face of superior forces. An average commander would have gone into winter quarters, conceding much of Alsace to Allied occupation, but Turenne did otherwise.

In early December, after the first snow fall, Turenne prepared to lead a brief and brilliant winter campaign. He chose only men and horses still in condition to conduct such a demanding exercise and took to the road by mid-month. Turenne used the Vosges to cover his march south and then east across the mountains to the assembly point at Belfort. Finally realizing that the French were on the move, the enemy scrambled to reassemble their troops, but Turenne hit them too fast. On 29 December he shattered enemy cavalry near Mulhouse and then advanced on Colmar, where the elector of Brandenburg hurriedly assembled an army of 30,000–40,000 men. Turenne

attacked with about 30,000 on 5 January 1675; after holding the enemy by feints, he outflanked the German position, taking Turkheim on the left. This victory forced the Germans to abandon Alsace.

The fighting began well for the French in 1675. In Flanders, the French carried off an extremely successful campaign to seize the line of the Meuse river and thus isolate the Spanish and Dutch from German aid coming from the east. First securing the neutrality of Liège, which had nearly gone over to the Spanish, the French then took Dinant, Huy, and Limbourg. Condé, now reduced by gout to riding in a carriage, acted as advisor to Louis, who had joined his army again. French success in that campaign put Louis in a strong position for the remainder of the war.

Yet, this year also removed two great French generals from the battlefield. In the summer of 1675, Turenne maneuvered along the Rhine to counter his old foe Montecuccoli, and on 27 July Turenne caught up with him near Sasbach. While the great French marshal reconnoitered the imperial position, a cannonball struck him down. Shaken by his death, the French recoiled, and Montecuccoli advanced into Alsace. Louis dispatched Condé south to take command in Alsace, where he contained the imperial advance without being able to drive the enemy back across the Rhine. Condé ended his military career with the fighting in Alsace, for his infirmities finally forced him to retire.

While the war saw its major action from Picardy to Alsace, subsidiary fronts along the Spanish border and on Sicily stretched Louis's resources. In 1674 Hermann Friedrich von Schomberg commanded a modest army against the Spanish along the Pyrenees, in Roussillon. This army was so meager that Louis called up militia from Languedoc to reinforce it. The French lost Bellegarde on the spine of the Pyrenees, and met defeat at Maureillas. Schomberg retook Bellegarde in July 1675, but did not much else because his army now dispatched troops for the campaign in Sicily. Fortunately for the French along the Pyrenees, Spanish forces there also sent troops to Sicily. In 1676 Navailles, who replaced Schomberg, assembled an army of 15,000 by using every means he could, including pulling men out of garrisons. However, his plans came to nought because, once again, Louis took troops from the Spanish front to fight in Sicily. The frustrated Navailles accomplished little during the rest of the war.

When the Messenians rebelled against new taxes imposed by their Spanish masters in July 1674, the Mediterranean became a major new front in the war. Tax revolt was a common form of uprising in the 17th century; in fact, the French would suffer a rising against war taxes in Bordeaux and Brittany during 1675. But if disturbances in France posed a threat, those among the enemy presented an opportunity. To help sustain the rebels Louis dispatched a fleet laden with wheat followed by a small body of French infantry that reached Messina on 1 January 1675, ferried over by six warships.

A month later the Duke of Vivonne arrived with an expeditionary force of 3,000 French troops and nine warships, accompanied by more vessels carrying supplies. Galleys from Marseilles also joined the gathering French fleet. From this point on, the French controlled the seas around Sicily. After more reinforcements arrived, Vivonne captured Augusta in August.

By the end of 1675 a Dutch fleet commanded by de Ruyter had reached Sicilian waters to support the Spanish. Admiral Abraham Duquesne (1610–88) sailed from Toulon and fought an inconclusive battle with de Ruyter on 8 January 1676 near the island of Stromboli. The two antagonists fought again on 22 April at the battle of Augusta, where the French won the day. During the furious cannonade de Ruyter's legs were smashed, and he died a week later. Some battered Dutch ships put into Palermo, where the French fleet, now under Vivonne, scored a notable success against the combined Dutch and Spanish fleet of 29 vessels and nine galleys on 2 June. Vivonne's victory broke Spanish naval power around Sicily, and the Dutch withdrew.

From the start, the primary French goal on Sicily had been simply to divert the Spanish, and in this game of attrition Louis invested as little as he could. Vivonne was able to undertake some operations through 1676 and 1677 that increased the French control in eastern Sicily, but his small army, never more than 6,000–7,000 troops, was insufficient to conquer the entire island. When it seemed that the English and their navy might enter the war against France in 1678, the French pulled out of Messina in March of that year.

The battles in Sicilian waters were not the only naval combats of the Dutch War. In fact, the first fighting had been an English naval attack against a Dutch convoy in the Channel on 23 March 1672. A few months later, on 7 June, de Ruyter, commanding

Duquesne, one of Louis's most successful sea commanders, achieved his greatest victory at Augusta in 1676 during French operations around Sicily. (Roger-Viollet)

Turenne's campaigns of 1674–1675

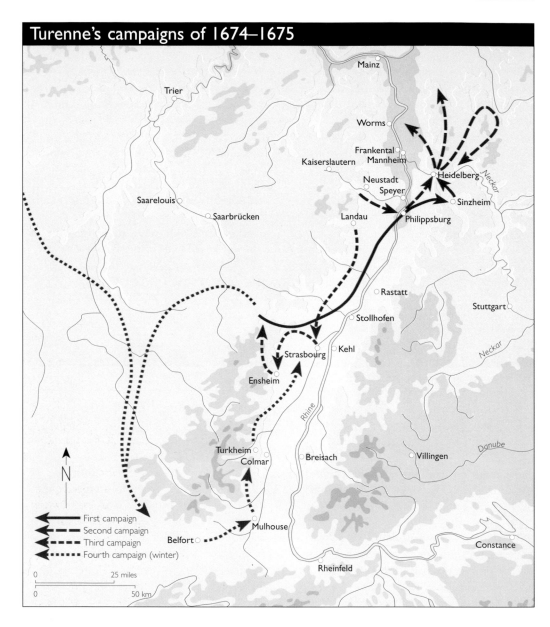

Mainz
Trier
Worms
Frankental
Kaiserslautern Mannheim
Neustadt
Heidelberg
Saarelouis Speyer
Saarbrücken Landau Sinzheim
Philippsburg
Rastatt
Stuttgart
Stollhofen
Kehl
Strasbourg
Ensheim
Rhine
Neckar
Neckar
Danube
Turkheim Breisach Villingen
Colmar
N
Mulhouse
Belfort
Constance
First campaign
Second campaign
Third campaign
Fourth campaign (winter)
Rheinfeld
0   25 miles
0   50 km

75 ships, surprised a combined English and French fleet at Sole Bay. After the French vessels under Count Jean d'Estrées withdrew, de Ruyter badly battered the English before having to pull back himself when English reinforcements arrived.

De Ruyter scored another victory exactly one year later when he mauled an English fleet under Prince Rupert in the Schoonveldt Channel. This success forestalled a planned English sea-borne invasion of Holland. Later, on 21 August 1673, de Ruyter triumphed

once more against a combined English and French fleet at the battle of Texel. This fight resulted both in bringing the Dutch East Indies fleet to port safely and in frustrating another attempted invasion by sea. De Ruyter's string of naval victories makes his later defeat by Duquesne off Sicily all the more remarkable.

After 1675 the war in Flanders and along the Rhine wound down. The disappearance of the old war-horses, Turenne and Condé, gave primary leverage to other of Louis's

At the battle of the Texel (21 August 1673) the great Dutch admiral, de Ruyter, defeated a combined English and French fleet. (AKG, Berlin)

advisors. Louvois and Vauban reinforced Louis's own tendency to concentrate on defending his new acquisitions rather than adding more. Before Turenne and Condé were gone, Louis had already taken important fortresses in Flanders and conquered Franche-Comté. In February 1674 he had sent Navailles with an army into that Spanish-held province, and in April Louis, accompanied by queen and court, joined the troops for the campaign, which the French wrapped up in June.

Louis's victories continued in Flanders. In 1676 the French took Condé, Bouchain, and Aire, while frustrating William's siege of Maastricht, where the arrival of an army commanded by Créqui compelled him to withdraw. During the next year, Louis's forces added Valenciennes, St Omer, Cambrai, and St Ghislain to their conquests. The field armies also fought an early battle on 11 April 1677 at Cassel, where Louis's brother, Philippe of Orleans, defeated William, who had advanced in hopes of relieving the siege of St Omer. In this campaign as with others, the supply magazines assembled through the efforts of Louvois allowed the French to take the field earlier in the year than was practical for the Dutch. Later in the year, the French frustrated another siege by William, who had to abandon his attempt to take Charleroi when Marshal Luxembourg arrived with a relief army in mid-August.

By 1678 Louis wanted to end the war as quickly as possible, and to this purpose he attacked and took Ghent on 12 March. Louis seized Ghent not to keep it, but to shock the Dutch. Ypres capitulated soon after. Louis presented peace terms to the Dutch in April, and they signed the Treaty of Nijmegen with the French on 10 August. In a most bitter irony, the word apparently did not reach the armies in the field, and Marshal Luxembourg and William III fought a particularly bitter, and ultimately unnecessary, battle at St Denis on 14 August.

Créqui conducted a notable campaign of maneuver along the Rhine during the last months of the war. But his brilliance did not alter the final balance at the peace table. The war gained territorial concessions for Louis. His original goal might have been frustrated, and he was unsuccessful in debasing the Dutch; however, he made off well. The Treaty of Nijmegen gave him Franche-Comté, a number of new towns on his north-east frontier, and Freiburg across the Rhine. He was now Louis the Great, the Sun King in full splendor.

The War of Reunions

Instead of basking in his new-won *gloire*, Louis used quasi-legal means backed by outright force to seize additional towns and lands. He believed that he was rationalizing his frontier simply to protect his domains, but his neighbors considered his actions those of an insatiable conqueror. Louis established French courts to hear his claims on disputed territory, and not surprisingly these Chambers of Reunions sided with him.

At the same time, Vauban repeatedly counseled Louis that the fortified city of Luxembourg, a Spanish possession, must be taken to protect France from future raids, so in July 1681 the French began to blockade the town. In September, Louis's troops swept down on Strasbourg and seized that city and its vital bridge. Louis gave up his blockade of Luxembourg in March 1682, but aggressive acts continued.

Driven to desperation, Spain declared war on France in October 1683. When the Austrian Habsburgs refused to join the Spanish, they faced Louis with only some Dutch aid. This brief War of the Reunions turned very brutal, particularly in the matter of imposing contributions and exacting

reprisals. The French had the upper hand and used it to grab Luxembourg, which they besieged and finally took on 3 June. Incidental to this conflict, a French fleet bombarded Genoa, 17–28 May, to chastise the city for allowing the Spanish to use their port and move through their territory.

On 15 August 1684 the warring parties signed the Truce of Ratisbon, by which Louis returned his conquests since August 1683, with the exception of Luxembourg, in return for a 20-year guarantee of his other gains, including Luxembourg and Strasbourg.

Louis was not done employing the sword to carve the world into the shape he desired. In October 1685 he revoked the Edict of Nantes, by which his grandfather, Henri IV, had promised toleration and security to French Protestants, or 'Huguenots.' For some years Louis had coerced conversions, often by garrisoning dragoons or other troops on Huguenot households, a practice known as the *dragonnades*. Now he compelled Huguenots to convert, but in opposition many fled France. Louis tried to shut down the flow into Italy by compelling the Duke of Savoy to attack his own benign Protestant Vaudois community in the Alps. Louis dispatched troops to lead the way in what became a virtual genocide of the Vaudois. It was Louis's most evil moment.

The Nine Years' War

Louis's obsession with making France invulnerable by keeping the gains of the Reunions led to a monumental miscalculation. Trusting that he could compel the Germans to accept the new status quo as a permanent settlement, he struck out in what was supposed to be a campaign of only a few months but which became the Nine Years' War.

Louis's main army invested Philippsburg on 27 September 1688. His son, the Dauphin, formally commanded these forces, but the Dauphin was a man of mediocre talent and limited experience, so Marshal Duras and Vauban attended the young

The magistrates of Strasbourg offering Louis XIV the keys to the city after his army seized the important city on 30 September 1681 as part of the Reunions. (Roger-Viollet)

prince. Philippsburg fell on 30 October, and the army marched on to Mannheim, which capitulated after a very brief siege on 11 November. In short order the French took Frankenthal and a number of towns that surrendered without resistance, including Oppenheim, Kaiserslautern, Heidelberg, and Speyer. The important fortress of Mainz accepted a French garrison.

Louis hoped to add Koblenz to his bag of towns, but its lord, the elector of Trier, refused to surrender the town. Unwilling to commit the troops necessary to take it by formal siege, Louis ordered it bombarded by mortars, the terror weapon of his day. Like 20th-century bombing from the air, mortar attack promised to destroy a town without requiring an army to occupy it. Mortar attack posed all the moral problems of air bombing, including the injustice of directly attacking women and children. Vauban opposed bombardment, but the French rained down shells on the city, gutting it in November.

Although Louis's military goals had been achieved, the Germans did not accede to his demands. Before long, Brandenburg, Hanover, Hesse-Kassel, Saxony, and Bavaria opposed him, to be joined by the forces of Leopold I and the Dutch. Two months of successful campaigning had not resulted in a quick victory, but had simply ignited a great war.

The Sun King was caught unprepared for this eventuality. He had not mobilized for a clash of such proportions, so he and his advisors opted to create a defensive barrier behind which the French could shelter and gear up for war. Louis ordered his troops to devastate the resources of the Palatinate, Baden, and Württemberg in order that no attacking army could subsist in the desert that this would create. The section 'World around war' deals with the resultant devastation of the Palatinate.

Once the French had created their Rhineland barrier, they fended off German ripostes as best they could, but Duras lacked the troops to defeat the new German armies that faced off against him in 1689. The most important military action of that year saw a German force commanded by Duke Charles of Lorraine surround and besiege Mainz in a long siege, which began in mid-July and lasted over seven weeks before the French capitulated on 8 September. Kaiserwörth and Bonn also fell to an army led by the elector of Brandenberg.

During 1689, the usual epicenter of Louis's wars, Flanders, rated as only secondary theater. The French and their Spanish and Dutch opponents maneuvered cautiously; Humières in command of the French devoted part of the fall to digging extensive defensive lines. It took some time for Flanders to heat up because Louis and William were occupied elsewhere, Louis along the Rhine and William in securing the English throne.

King James II wore the crown, but he lacked wisdom, and that lack cost him everything during the Glorious Revolution. His open conversion to Catholicism by the early 1670s was bad enough, but his second marriage to Mary of Este, a Papist, produced a male heir in 1687 who would perpetuate a Catholic dynasty, and this was a prospect the English could not countenance.

The Dutch Protestant champion William had claims to the throne himself as a grandson of Charles I and through his wife, Mary, a Protestant daughter of James II and heir presumptive at the time of her marriage to William. The Stadtholder now ventured to be king, and on 5 November 1688 he landed

in England with troops. This was an invasion, but one welcomed by many. James fled, and William and Mary ascended to the throne in April 1689. Louis's involvement in his new continental war helped clear the way for William; in fact, the French court expected turmoil in the British Isles to occupy William for a long time and thus neutralize England and the United Provinces. However, William immediately entered the lists against Louis, bringing England with him.

Louis tried to intervene on James's behalf to resist William's efforts to secure Ireland. Louis called upon his navy to oppose William, but while shuttling troops to Ireland, it did not intervene strategically. At Bantry Bay, Château-Renault won a limited victory against Torrington on 11 May 1689, which allowed the French to land troops and supplies. The most notable triumph of Louis's navy came the next year when Tourville defeated an Anglo-Dutch fleet under Torrington on 10 July 1690 at the battle of Beachy Head. But the consequences of the victory reveal the limited importance of naval battles during the Nine Years' War. Tourville enjoyed temporary dominance of the Channel, but did nothing with it, and the Allies quickly replaced the six ships they had lost.

The French would have done better to use their naval power to interdict English shipping from England to Ireland. William had been able to cross over to Ireland with a sizeable army; there he won the critical battle of the Boyne on the day after Beachy Head. French intervention in Ireland was more an attempt to occupy William than it was a full-force effort to maintain James II. The fall of Limerick on 13 October 1691 ended Louis's Irish diversion.

The naval war outlasted the Irish adventure, but Louis would give up French dreams of a navy to match the English and Dutch before the Nine Years' War had run its course. It would be tempting to say that French naval power received its deathblow when Admirals Russell and Rooke defeated Tourville at the battle of Barfleur–La Hogue on 29 May–3 June 1692.

Supposed to clear the Channel for a French descent on England in support of James II, Tourville sailed under inflexible orders to engage the Allies at sea, even though the Toulon squadron had failed to arrive to beef up his own fleet. The Allied fleet outgunned Tourville 8,980 cannon to 3,142. Nonetheless, Tourville attacked the superior Allied force, and during the fighting of Barfleur the French did well, losing no ships. Yet when Tourville broke off action and withdrew, he met disaster. The lack of deep-water ports on the Channel forced Tourville to run for St Malo and Brest, but 15 of his vessels, including the bloated *Soleil Royal*, sought shelter under French batteries at Cherbourg and La Hogue, where they were burned. Loss at Barfleur–La Hogue forestalled invasion plans, but it did not scuttle the fleet. Tourville, in fact, won the battle of Lagos a year later, on 27 June 1693.

Soon, however, the fleet fell victim to the need to concentrate the monarchy's investment on the ever-larger army. Famine in 1693–94, which caused human misery on a grand scale while diminishing crown revenues, helped to bring matters to a head. While the French had fixated on the idea of the fleet as a means of guarding the coast from Allied incursions, the fact that Vauban employed only land forces to repel an Allied descent on Brest at Camaret in June 1694 suggested that the army, both regulars and militia, could protect the coast equally well at far less cost. At this point, the French switched emphasis to attacking Allied commerce in *guerre de course*, and from 1695 there were no major fleet operations in the Atlantic.

The Nine Years' War took on the outlines of Louis's other struggles, as the main seat of action returned to Flanders in 1690. That year Louis entrusted command of this theater to Marshal Luxembourg, who fought his tactical masterpiece, the battle of Fleurus, on 1 July. With William III in Ireland, Prince Waldeck commanded the main Allied army. Luxembourg outmaneuvered Waldeck in June, unexpectedly crossing the Sambre river on a pontoon bridge and quickly coming upon the Allied army posted on the high ground near Fleurus. Luxembourg led about

35,000 men at Fleurus, and Waldeck probably mustered a few thousand more.

On the morning of the battle, Luxembourg used the lie of the land to hide his advance against his static enemy. Instead of coming directly at Waldeck, Luxembourg took the extreme risk of splitting his army in two and attacking the enemy simultaneously from both flanks. Crushed between the two halves of the French army, Waldeck's troops lost about 6,000 dead, 5,000 wounded, and 8,000 prisoners, adding up to a casualty rate of 50 percent.

If the battle tactics were truly Napoleonic, the pursuit was far from it. Instead of trying to eliminate Waldeck's entire army or harry it out of Flanders, Luxembourg accepted the parameters of contemporary warfare and, instead, allowed Waldeck to seek safety in Brussels while the French imposed war taxes on a broad swatch of now-undefended territory.

During 1691, William III reappeared as stadtholder and king in Flanders, but Luxembourg scored repeated successes over him. Exploiting the French advantage of starting the campaign season early, Louis took Mons in a siege that lasted from 15 March until 10 April. That summer Louvois, upon whose bureaucratic mastery so much depended, including the stockpiling of magazines, died. His successors never equaled his abilities. Later that fall, on 19 September, Luxembourg attacked and bested the rear of the Allied army at Leuze. This force was in the process of withdrawing for quarters, and William had handed over command to the unfortunate Waldeck.

The next year witnessed one of the most notable sieges of Louis's reign. Namur guarded the confluence of the Sambre and Meuse rivers; it was, thus, a naturally important fortress. Louis attended this siege, which employed a besieging army of 60,000 troops with a covering army of 60,000 commanded by Luxembourg. Vauban directed the siege, while the great Dutch engineer Menno van Coehoorn conducted the defense with a garrison of about 6,000 troops. It was a duel of giants. The

fortifications of Namur included a town, built upon the flat land on the left bank of the Sambre, and a citadel perched upon high ground on the left bank, wedged between the Sambre and the Meuse.

French cavalry invested Namur on the night of 25–26 May 1692, and after digging lines of circumvallation, the French opened the attack trenches on the night of 29–30 May. The town capitulated quickly on condition that its garrison could cross the Sambre to the citadel and that the French would not bombard the citadel from the

LEFT The heavily decorated stern of Louis's largest warship, *Le Soleil Royal*, or the *Royal Sun*. The symbolism of Apollo's chariot rising from the sea refers to the sun, Louis's emblem. *Le Soleil Royal* was burned at the battle of La Hogue in 1692. (Roger-Viollet)

BELOW At the battle of La Hogue in 1692, the Anglo-Dutch fleet destroyed French vessels not during the open sea fight, but as French vessels sought shelter in French ports and were there set alight by allied sailors who approached in launches. (Ann Ronan Picture Library)

town. These conditions were accepted on 5 June, and a truce intervened until the morning of 7 June, when the fighting resumed.

The real fight raged at the heights. Vauban set up batteries; Coehoorn forced him to move them. Vauban drove trenches forward; Coehoorn built works on the reverse slope so that they would be sheltered until the French were upon them. In a dramatic gesture, Coehoorn ordered his grave dug to symbolize his commitment to defend Namur to the end. As it was, Coehoorn was wounded during the siege. Finally the forces in the citadel capitulated on 30 June and marched out with the honors of war on 1 July.

Later that summer, William sought to engage the French on difficult ground to neutralize their superior cavalry, and he succeeded in surprising Luxembourg's army across such wooded terrain at Steenkerque on 3 August. However, the French regained their composure and fought off the Allied

The battle of Fleurus

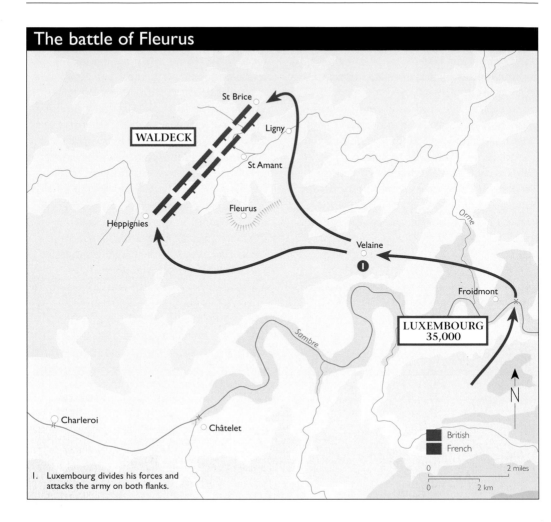

1. Luxembourg divides his forces and attacks the army on both flanks.

At Fleurus Luxembourg led 35,000 men against Waldeck's few thousand more men. Waldeck's army was positioned on the high ground near Fleurus when Luxembourg made his unexpected attack, having crossed the Sambre river by pontoon bridge. He split his army and thus attacked both flanks of his enemy at the same time. The risk paid off and Waldeck lost up to 50 percent as casualties before retreating to safety in Brussels.

assault, forcing William to abandon the battlefield late in the day.

Louis's army continued to grow as a whole, and the field forces commanded by Luxembourg in 1693 swelled in proportion. Yet larger forces did not lead to decisive campaigns. Most of the campaign season that year in Flanders saw the usual thrust and parry. Early on Louis joined his army for an attempt on Liège, but the King became ill. Louis's infirmity so delayed the French that

they lost their opportunity to take the enemy off guard, and the plan had to be scrapped. Time had caught up with Louis, who now, aged 54, judged himself too old to join his troops in the field.

On 29 July, Luxembourg at the head of 80,000 troops attacked William in his entrenched camp around Neerwinden. Detachments had reduced William's army to 50,000, and Luxembourg hoped to gain from his numerical advantage. Luxembourg won the day, capturing so many enemy flags to hang in triumph at Notre Dame that he was called the *Tapissier de Notre Dame*. Yet this victory, bought at the cost of 14,000 Allied casualties and 7,000–8,000 French, had little immediate result beyond attrition. Soon after the battle, William gathered back dispersed elements of his forces to restore his army.

Luxembourg went on to besiege Charleroi, investing the fortress on 10 September and taking it a month later.

Famine so exhausted the resources of the contending parties that 1694 brought no great battles or sieges in Flanders. The most significant action came in September, when the small fortress of Huy fell to the Allies.

The fall of Huy made it easier for William to pursue his main object for 1695 – the retaking of Namur. The theater witnessed a change of characters this year. Louis did not travel with his armies after 1693, and Luxembourg, his undefeated marshal, died in January 1695. With his passing, Marshal Villeroi rose to the command of French forces in Flanders. Villeroi's talents fell far short of Luxembourg's, so Louis tried to keep him on a tighter leash. Not surprisingly, Louis emphasized the defensive and ordered Boufflers to construct elaborate defensive lines running between the Lys and the Scheldt. To do so Boufflers mobilized some

20,000 peasant laborers, or pioneers. With such a massive workforce the job only took a week, 6–13 April.

When Villeroi advocated more aggressive operations in June, Louis told him to hold the lines: 'One must defend my country foot by foot.' But defend it all he could not. While William occupied Villeroi, the elector of Brandenberg led another Allied force to invest Namur on 1 July. Boufflers commanded the defending garrison of about 13,000. William then marched on Namur, where the besieging forces and the army of observation now totaled about 80,000. Coehoorn reversed his role of 1692 and conducted the attack, while Boufflers led an active defense and only capitulated on 5 September. The fighting would not end for two more years, but the

This view of the 1695 siege of Namur by allied forces, shows the way the heights across the Sambre dominated the town. (Ann Ronan Picture Library)

fall of Namur was the last great military action of the Nine Years' War in the Spanish Netherlands.

Other fronts consumed lesser efforts. The French and Allies stationed armies along the Moselle and the Rhine, but the operations there declined in importance after the initial clashes of 1688–89. Much of French maneuvering had as its goal allowing French armies to subsist off German resources. The Marquis de Quincy, a contemporary commentator, praised de Lorge's campaign of 1691: 'Marshal de Lorge found the means to make the army of the king live on the

enemies' country during the entire campaign, to take from them large contributions and to subsist at their expense.'

In 1692 the German forces outnumbered de Lorge's, so he conducted a more modest campaign, still ravaging and raiding areas along the Rhine. The next year, with an

army that reached 45,000 men, de Lorge, accompanied by the Dauphin, took Heidelberg, 21–22 May. They then faced off along the Neckar against a German host commanded by Baden, but no battle resulted.

Little of note occurred in 1694 or 1695, apart from the by now usual marches and raids. During the 1695 campaign, Joyeuse replaced de Lorge, who had become ill. As so often occurred during the wars of Louis XIV, armies on one front were employed as reinforcements for armies elsewhere, and Joyeuse detached troops to Flanders to aid in opposing the Allied offensive there.

The war in Catalonia was largely a sideshow for Louis. It was an amphibious front, where naval operations would be necessary to assist in the seizing of coastal towns and the greatest prize of all, Barcelona. Until 1695, the Duke de Noailles commanded the French army in Roussillon and Catalonia, but he normally led only modest forces, which topped out at about 12,000 in 1690 and 10,000 in 1691. As in the previous wars, troops were pulled out of Spain in 1692 and 1693 to reinforce fighting elsewhere in the Mediterranean, this time against Victor Amadeus.

Only in 1694, when the other fronts were relatively quiescent, did Spain figure large, but even then the French invested only about 26,000 troops on this front. Rosas had fallen to the French the previous year, and now the French drove deeper into Catalonia, defeating the Spanish at the battle of the Ter on 27 May and then taking the coastal town of Palamos, which capitulated on 10 June; Gerona fell on 29 June. However, the arrival of an Allied fleet off Barcelona in August forestalled an intended French siege. The continued presence of the Allied fleet under Russell in 1695 also ruled out a French siege the next year.

In a dramatic contrast to war along the Rhine and the Pyrenees, the fighting in

French troops commanded by Marshal Luxembourg attack William III's entrenched camp at the battle of Neerwinden, 29 July 1693. (Roger-Viollet)

Martin's painting of the 1692 siege of Namur, a triumph for Vauban, provides an excellent view of the low-lying town of Namur with its defensive bastions and the citadel on the hills between the Meuse and the Sambre. (AKG, Berlin)

northern Italy witnessed impressive
maneuvers and pitched battles. It is
important to recognize that there was no
single style of campaigning during the wars
of the Sun King, but that the size of armies,
the geography, and the prevalence of
fortifications had considerable influence, to
say nothing of the character of command.
This front gave France one of its more
unusual military heroes, Marshal Catinat,
who was an anomaly among marshals
because he did not hail from the upper
reaches of the aristocracy but descended
from a modest family of legal and
administrative functionaries.

The actual fighting did not break out until
Victor Amadeus II, Duke of Savoy, joined the
Allies in the spring of 1690. Catinat, at the
head of a small army of only 12,000, defeated
the duke at the battle of Staffarde on
18 August, inflicting 4,000 killed, wounded,
and captured. Reinforced in 1691, Catinat
took Nice between 24 March and 2 April with
the loss of only 100 men. He then fought
along the Po, taking Carmagnola. However,
imperial reinforcements raised the size of the
Duke's forces to 45,000 men, and Catinat had
to pull back, losing Carmagnola in October.
However, another smaller French army under
Hoguette crossed the little St Bernard and
scored a series of victories in the Val d'Aosta.

During 1692 Catinat had to deal with a
stark numerical disadvantage, having only
15,000–16,000 troops for much of the year,
when Victor Amadeus mustered 50,000. Yet
this did not overwhelm Catinat, who was
able to maintain the French hold on Susa and
Pinerolo. The next year saw a more equal
confrontation, although Catinat began 1693
again at a numerical disadvantage. However,
when additional reinforcements reached
Catinat late in the campaign season, he
frustrated Victor Amadeus's siege of Pinerolo
and then defeated him on 4 October at
the battle of Marsaglia, which faced off
40,000 French against 36,000 Allies. After
this, the next year was comparatively quiet.

The war wound down quickly during the
final two years. The Duke of Savoy was the
first major partner to abandon the coalition.

Marshal Boufflers at the defense of Lille in 1708. He
became a hero by holding Lille against Eugene and
Marlborough for nearly four months even though he had
to capitulate in December. (Roger-Viollet)

He had been badly bruised by the French
forces deployed against him, but he took
advantage of Louis's need to extricate
himself from the war by cutting a deal with
the Sun King, a deal that gave the duke
peace and possession. In 1695 the French
and Savoyards staged a campaign to
eliminate the French hold on Casale, a target
of Savoyard action for some time. Louis's
forces agreed to give up Casale after a sham
siege, and the fortress yielded on 9 July. It
was then demolished and handed back to
the Duke of Mantua, who had sold the
fortress to Louis back in 1681. In 1696 Victor
Amadeus formally concluded peace with
Louis through the Treaty of Turin signed on
29 August. By this treaty Louis agreed to
abandon Pinerolo as well.

Little action disturbed the Spanish
Netherlands during 1696 and 1697, as peace
approached. Villeroi in Flanders and
Boufflers on the Meuse commanded a total
force of about 125,000 men in 1696, against
which William III, the elector of Bavaria, and
the Landgrave of Hesse could martial about
equal numbers. At the start of the campaign
season in 1697 the French took Ath on
5 June, but representatives of Louis and
William were bargaining hard for peace. The
opposing sides marched to and fro along the
Rhine, but undertook little serious combat in
1696. The Prince of Baden was able to take
Ebernberg in a siege during September 1697,
just before the end of the war. In Spain, even
though the English fleet departed from Cadiz
and sailed north in the spring of 1696, the
French did not make an attempt on
Barcelona that year. However, with the
assistance of a French fleet under the
command of d'Estrées, Vendôme took
Barcelona in the summer of 1697, the final
major action of the war.

On 20 September representatives of
France, the United Provinces, England, and
Spain signed the Treaty of Ryswick, and the

emperor accepted the treaty several weeks later on 30 October. Louis had to hand back Luxembourg and certain other of the Reunions, yet he kept Strasbourg and had a treaty guaranteeing his borders: above all, he regained peace.

The War of the Spanish Succession

Louis tried to avoid a confrontation over the Spanish Succession, but the will of Carlos II left him little choice. Louis's fault lay not in accepting the will, but in his imperious actions after accepting it. The actual fighting began in Italy during the summer of 1701, where the great imperial general Prince Eugene of Savoy defeated a French army under Tessé at the battle of Carpi on 9 July. Eugene next handed Marshal Villeroi a drubbing at Chiari. Eugene's attempted *coup de main* to seize Cremona on 1 February 1702 failed, but in a bizarre set of circumstances he captured Villeroi himself. These actions in Italy were only a prelude to full-scale war, but they foreshadowed campaigns to come; the near invincibility of the French army was at an end.

William III hammered together another Grand Alliance between England, the United Provinces, and the Emperor on 7 September 1701. However, this was William's last major political act, for he died in March 1702. William had been a great politician and diplomat, but a mediocre general; his death passed command of the English and Dutch army to the far more able hands of the duke of Marlborough.

Once again, the primary theater of the war was Flanders: that is, the Spanish Netherlands. At first this was because Louis intended to hold it for his grandson, Philip V, but later in the war, as Marlborough pushed the French further and further south, Louis concentrated his forces there to protect his own domains and the road to Paris. More than in any of the Sun King's other conflicts, the French depended on defensive lines during the War of the Spanish Succession.

The French constructed a series of them in the Spanish Netherlands, from the lines of Brabant facing the Dutch border at the start of the fighting to the Ne Plus Ultra lines of 1711. French and Germans dug other lines along the Alsatian front. Such defensive works were long and sophisticated, and while sometimes outflanked or breached, they proved their worth.

Marlborough and the Allies took a handful of forts along the Meuse and the Rhine in 1702, including Kaiserwerth, Venlo, and Roermond, but he did not crack the main French lines. In fact, the King's grandson, the Duke of Burgundy, in nominal command of the French forces, and the trusty Marshal Boufflers made scant attempt to defend these first fortresses. Marlborough and Coehoorn also took Liège in October; this was a great prize, but the French committed so many troops to garrisons on Spanish lands in Flanders that they could not send a large field army to defend Liège. In 1703 Villeroi took command of French troops in Flanders, where he frustrated Marlborough's attempt to take Antwerp, although the Allies managed to seize Huy.

The French also held off the Allies in Germany. The aging Marshal Catinat led French troops to raise the siege of Landau by Louis of Baden. Baden blocked Catinat, and Landau eventually succumbed in September 1702; nonetheless, its garrison held out so long that it made any other Allied operation along the Rhine impossible. Meanwhile, Catinat dispatched Villars to support the operations of Louis's ally, Elector Max Emanuel of Bavaria. Villars gave Louis a victory over Baden at the Battle of Friedelingen in the Black Forest on 14 October. At this point, Claude Hector Villars rated simply as one of Louis's several marshals; the Sun King would take years to recognize Villars as his most talented field commander.

In 1703 Villars marched his troops to the Danube to operate with Max Emanuel, who had taken Ulm, Neustadt, and Ratisbon. Louis ordered Villars to make the enemy pay for as much as 40 percent of his campaign by imposing contributions on enemy German populations. Villars and Max Emanuel defeated an imperial army under Styrum at the battle of Höchstädt on 20 September, but the strong and rough-edged marshal could not abide Max Emanuel, and Villars asked to be relieved of his command in this theater.

Meanwhile, French operations back along the Rhine went well in 1703, as the Duke of Burgundy and Marshal Tallard took Breisach in September. Tallard next besieged Landau, and when a German army approached to relieve the fortress, Tallard came out from his lines and defeated the Germans at the battle of Speyer on 15 November. Landau was soon in French hands again.

In Italy, the very capable duke Vendôme faced Starembourg, as Eugene had been called back to Vienna. Vendôme attempted to link up with Max Emanuel through the Tyrol, but arrived too late, voiding the Bavarian plan. The French then had to march south quickly, however, because Victor Amadeus, who had begun the war as a French ally, switched sides to join the Grand Alliance. Vendôme surrounded, disarmed, and took prisoner most of the Duke's forces in Lombardy in September, and the Duke began a losing battle against the French over the next two years that would leave him with little but his capital at Turin.

Thus the first few years of the war seemed to go reasonably well for Louis, but the tide turned sharply against him during 1704–06, which were years of triumph for Marlborough and Eugene. In 1704 Marlborough brought much of his army from Flanders to the Danube, where he combined with Eugene against the French and the Bavarians. Marlborough's march with 20,000 troops began in mid-May and covered 250 miles (400 km) to reach the Danube five weeks later. Rather that living off the country in Napoleonic fashion, Marlborough's troops ate food supplied to them at the end of each day's march by diligent commissioners.

Things heated up immediately with Marlborough's arrival. His forces stormed the Bavarian entrenched camp at Donauwörth on 2 July, taking the fortifications by *coup de main* since he lacked siege artillery. Now Marshal Tallard and Prince Eugene, who had been dueling along the Rhine, both shifted their armies to the Danube.

On 13 August the combined armies of Marlborough and Eugene attacked the Franco–Bavarian forces encamped with their right flank on the Danube at the village of Blenheim. The opposing armies each numbered about 60,000 troops. Here Marlborough scored his signature victory, by threatening the flanks of Tallard's army, while Eugene battled with Marsin and the elector. When Tallard reinforced his flanks with infantry, and thus weakened his center, Marlborough broke the center with his cavalry and shattered the French. Tallard ended the day as Marlborough's prisoner. The crushing Allied victory at Blenheim did not decide the fate of the war, but it ended the war on the Danube. On 7 November the elector's wife – he had become an exile – signed the Treaty of Ilbersheim allowing the imperial occupation of Bavaria.

From the day he had taken the reins of power in 1661, Louis had not suffered such a defeat; Blenheim stunned the French court. Yet such shocks were to become common. Back in Flanders during 1705, Marlborough did not repeat his startling success, as the French and Allied armies dueled with little effect. However, in 1706, Louis, who interpreted 1705 as French success, instructed Marshal Villeroi to confront Marlborough head on at the beginning of the campaign season. Marlborough was happy to oblige, and fought Villeroi around the village of Ramillies on 23 May; again the opposing forces each brought about 60,000 troops to the field. Marlborough repeated his tactics of Blenheim at Ramillies, for after battling at the flanks, he delivered the fatal blow with a cavalry attack on the French center.

Because it came so early in the year, victory at Ramillies presented Marlborough with a great opportunity to exploit his victory. He reported: 'We have now the whole summer before us, and with the

The blunt and hard-fighting Marshal Villars rescued French fortunes in the War of the Spanish Succession. Villars was on a par with Turenne and Luxembourg as Louis's greatest battlefield generals. (AKG, Berlin)

blessing of God, I shall make the best use of it.' A series of towns that were ripe for the taking, not boasting strong fortifications and prepared garrisons, fell like ten-pins: Louvain, Brussels, Malines, Lierre, Ghent, Alost, Damme, Oudenarde, Bruges, and Antwerp. Yet when Marlborough came up against a strong fortress at Dendermonde, he had to wait two weeks for his siege train to arrive. Nonetheless, victory at Ramillies won him control over most of Flanders.

Louis also lost his hold in northern Italy in 1706. After the Duke of Savoy had been reduced to holding his capital at Turin, the French closed in on that city in 1705. Vendôme defeated Eugene at the Battle of Cassano on 16 August of that year, and in September La Feuillade began preliminary siege operations around Turin, but stopped because it was too late in the year. The formal siege of Turin began in mid-May 1706. Back in France, Vauban, too old to go to the front, loudly disapproved of the way La Feuillade conducted the siege, which dragged on for months.

At the end of August, Eugene arrived with a relief army and joined forces with those of the duke of Savoy, who had escaped from Turin in June. The besieging French were now besieged themselves, caught between the large garrison of the town and Eugene and Victor Amadeus, with about 30,000 troops. At the battle of Turin on 7 September, the French army of 41,000 troops led by La Feuillade and the duke of Orléans, advised by Marsin, suffered utter defeat. The French now abandoned northern Italy; in 1707 the Convention of Milan neutralized Italy for the remainder of the war.

Turmoil at home accompanied defeat across the borders of France. Louis had feared a Huguenot uprising in France at least since the Revocation of the Edict of Nantes, and such a revolt struck Languedoc around

Nîmes and through the hills of the Cévennes in the summer of 1702. The rebels, called Camisards after the white shirts they wore, answered the call of local 'prophets.' Harsh policies on the part of Catholic authorities provoked violence by the Camisards. The fighting was sporadic but particularly brutal. When the local military commander proved unable to quell the disturbances, Louis dispatched Marshal Montreval to take over in February 1703. Montreval broke the back of the insurgency, finally resorting to systematic devastation to accomplish it. The next year Marshal Villars replaced Montreval and through a combination of carrot and stick brought peace in 1704. Instances of violence sputtered on after 1704, but the area was essentially pacified.

Louis enjoyed some success after his *annus horribilis* of 1706. The main Allied project for 1707 was an invasion of Provence, so the forces that might have aided Marlborough were diverted to the Mediterranean. In Flanders, the French entrenched new lines, but neither battle nor major siege pitted the adversaries against each other. Louis eventually dispatched troops from Flanders to buttress Provence against the Allied invasion. Even though Eugene commanded the advancing Allied forces, they ultimately failed. He and Victor Amadeus hoped to take the French port of Toulon, and they began formal siege operations there on 26 July; however the French under Marshal Tessé actively resisted their efforts, compelling Eugene to withdraw after a month.

Along the Rhine, Marshal Villars fought an archetypal campaign in 1707, designed more to make war feed war than to achieve any grand strategic goal. Louis instructed Villars that the collection of contributions in Germany should rank as the Marshal's 'principal and sole object.' However, Villars could not simply ravage at will; he had to break through German opposition, which at this time was concentrated along a prepared defensive position, the lines of Stollhofen First constructed in 1703 and later reinforced, these lines stretched about nine miles (15 km) from Stollhofen on the Rhine

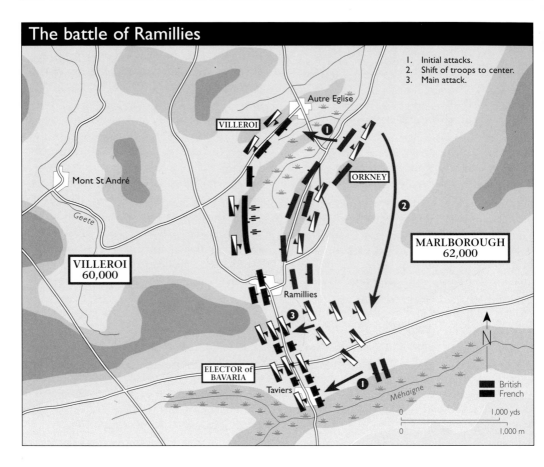

The battle of Ramillies

1. Initial attacks.
2. Shift of troops to center.
3. Main attack.

Autre Eglise

VILLEROI

Mont St André

ORKNEY

Geete

VILLEROI
60,000

MARLBOROUGH
62,000

Ramillies

ELECTOR of
BAVARIA

Taviers

Méhaigne

British
French

0   1,000 yds

0   1,000 m

N

As at Blenheim, Marlborough began the battle by attacking the flanks of the army under Villeroi and the elector of Bavaria. When these initial assaults drew the attention and reserves of the Franco-Bavarian force, Marlborough skillfully shifted cavalry from his right flank to reinforce his center, where he broke the Franco–Bavarian center with a decisive cavalry action.

to the mountains just east of Bühl. These lines had proved impregnable for years, but by very clever maneuvering Villars distracted and outflanked the enemy, taking the lines virtually without loss. When the opposing commander, fearing that Villars would attack Bavaria, fell back, Villars was free to harvest German resources. Württemberg alone conceded to pay contributions of 2,200,000 *livres*.

But while 1707 finished with French success in Provence and along the Rhine, the next year brought renewed disaster in Flanders. Louis entrusted his army there to the duke Vendôme with his grandson, the

Duke of Burgundy, as titular commander. As had Louis himself and the Dauphin before him, the Duke of Burgundy had served at the head of an army as early as 1702, without ill effect, but in 1708 he would lose a battle for his grandfather. Vendôme skillfully won back Ghent and Bruges during the first week of July, but Marlborough, again reinforced by Prince Eugene, countered at the battle of Oudenarde on 11 July.

Unlike Marlborough's other victories, Oudenarde was a meeting engagement, as the armies, now fielding about 80,000 troops each, came up piecemeal into the fight. Vendôme, in command of the advanced French right, believed he could beat the Allies, but his repeated appeals to the young duke to bring up the French left went unanswered. Vendôme's wing was eventually nearly surrounded, and he had to withdraw as best he could.

Defeat at Oudenarde cost Louis the rest of Flanders and threatened a collapse along the frontier, but to advance into northern France, the Allies would have to take Lille, one of Vauban's masterpieces. Louis entrusted its defense to Marshal Boufflers in command of a garrison of 14,000. Eugene attacked the city with 35,000 troops, while Marlborough stood off with an army of observation numbering 75,000 troops. The Allies invested Lille on 14 August, but Boufflers conducted such an expert and aggressive defense that he held them off for months. He offered to surrender the town on 22 October, then withdrew his troops into the citadel, which only capitulated on 8 December. The garrison marched out with well-deserved honors two days later. The defense of Lille held the front while the French regrouped and rebuilt new lines to continue the war.

The contest in Spain, the ultimate reason for the war, seesawed back and forth. Fighting did not begin across the Pyrenees until 1704, the year that the Austrian claimant, Archduke Charles, reached Lisbon. An Anglo-Dutch naval expedition took Gibraltar on 3 August 1704 and then held off a French fleet at the battle of Velez-Málaga. In October 1705 the Allies took Barcelona after a siege that cut off the city from land and sea. Importantly, Leopold I died in 1705, to be succeeded by Joseph I. There was no reason to believe that Joseph I would not have a long reign, but should he die young, Archduke Charles would succeed him.

Philip V at Madrid would have to face challenges on two fronts, from Portugal, where the English enjoyed an alliance and could invade from the east, and from the Mediterranean, where naval preeminence allowed the Allies to sustain operations from the coast. For most of the year, the campaign of 1706 brought news as apocalyptic as that coming from Flanders and Italy. Philip V mounted an unsuccessful attempt to retake Barcelona, and in devoting so much to Barcelona, the Franco–Spanish forces were weak elsewhere. When an Allied army advanced from Portugal to take Madrid, Philip had to flee his capital in June. Just days after the Allies, led by Galway and Das

Minas, marched into Madrid, they also took Saragossa, on 29 June. But the Allies proved unable to keep their hold on Madrid in the face of growing Franco–Spanish opposition and at the end of a long supply line, so they withdrew to Valencia, and Philip reentered his capital on 4 October.

In 1707 the Franco–Spanish forces rebounded to score important victories. Marshal Berwick, an illegitimate son of James II, advanced against Galway and beat him at the battle of Almanza on 25 April, a defeat that cost the Allies Valencia. Almanza did not win the war in Spain, but it surely set things on a different course. Valencia fell to the French on 8 May and Saragossa on 26 May. The Catalan town of Lerida capitulated to the Franco–Spanish forces on 14 October. Meanwhile, near the Portuguese border, Ciudad Rodrigo also passed into Philip's hands on 4 October after a siege of nearly three weeks. By the close of 1707 Philip held most of Spain.

The French made modest gains in Catalonia during 1708, an otherwise rather uneventful year in Spain; Franco–Spanish armies also did little more than maintain the status quo in 1709. The next year threatened disaster at the outset and ended in triumph for Philip V. As an effort to encourage peace negotiations, Louis had withdrawn his generals and forces from Spain, and Philip V could not handle the Allied army led by its commander-in-chief, Starhemberg. That general defeated the Spanish at the Battle of Almenara on 27 July, won again at the Battle of Saragossa on 20 August, and finally took Madrid on 21 September.

However, with his hopes for peace dashed, Louis recommitted to Spain, sending Vendôme and reinforcements. With this pressure, Starhemberg retreated from Madrid and made for the coast with Vendôme on his heels. Vendôme caught the rear guard of the Allied army and defeated it on 9 December 1710 at the battle of Brihuega, and the next day Vendôme took on Starhemberg and the main body. This costly battle of Villa Viciosa ended in a tactical draw; Vendôme pushed Starhemberg from his position, but withdrew

France was blest with only two ports that could accommodate a fleet of warships. Toulon, shown here, was her great sailing port on the Mediterranean. (AKG, Berlin)

from the battlefield himself at the end of the day. Yet the consequences of the fight proved horrendous for Starhemberg, who abandoned his artillery and baggage in a rush for Catalonia. The French diplomat Torcy said of these battles, 'No matter what,

never has a victory been more complete, and this day will change the face of affairs in Spain and at the same time those of Europe.'

The tide of war in the northeast began to shift in Louis's favor in 1709, although the year began with the blackest expectations. Not only had Oudenarde won the enemy Flanders, but famine stalked France. After a poor harvest in 1708, the winter of 1708–09 brought the worst natural disaster of Louis's

troops to drive Philip from his throne. Louis, as king and as grandfather, balked at this last condition, and on 12 June 1709 he issued two letters to the French explaining his actions in continuing the war. The absolute monarch appealed to popular opinion.

Resolved to continue the struggle, Louis now put his best commander, Villars, on the paramount front, Flanders. It had taken him too long to separate the wheat from the chaff among his generals, but at last Mme de Maintenon, the morganatic wife of the Sun King, could write, 'We finally have a general who has faith in the soldier, in the fate of France, and in himself.' The task facing Villars seemed insurmountable. While trying to keep an army together with little money and little food, his men poorly supplied and unshod, he had to confront the invincible Marlborough and his extraordinary comrade Prince Eugene.

Marlborough continued his conquering ways by besieging Tournai. The garrison hoped to occupy Marlborough and Eugene as long as possible there, and, in fact, Tournai held out from late June to 3 September. However, instead of ending the year's campaigning by seizing that fortress, the Allies planned to besiege Mons. Louis, who had been reluctant to commit his troops to battle, now authorized Villars to engage Marlborough: 'Should Mons follow the fate of Tournai, our case is undone; you are by every means in your power to relieve the garrison; the cost is not to be considered; the salvation of France is at stake.' Villars with about 75,000 troops took up defensive positions around Malplaquet, and on 11 September, Marlborough and Eugene attacked with combined forces totaling roughly 86,000 men and 100 cannon.

In attacks on the French right, Dutch battalions suffered horrendous losses, but the French held. On the French left, Marlborough's flanking attack so worried Villars that he stripped his center of most of its infantry and personally led the fight on the left. While he was leading a charge, an enemy musket ball shattered his knee, and he had to be carried from

reign, an intense cold that struck down people and animals while killing trees, vines, and winter wheat. Louis instructed his diplomats to accept almost any conditions to gain peace; however, the Allies asked for too much. They insisted that Louis withdraw his support for Philip V and abandon a series of fortresses as a display of good faith, while all the Allies offered in return was a two-month truce. Moreover, Louis must commit French

French success at the battle of Villa Viciosa (10 December, 1710) spelled doom for the allied cause in Spain. Here the talented duke of Vendôme presents captured flags to Philip V, the young king of Spain. (Ann Ronan Picture Library)

the field, so Boufflers assumed command. Marlborough once again relied on a determined cavalry attack to break the weakened French center. At about 1.30 pm, he gathered as many as 30,000 cavalry. Charge and countercharge thundered back and forth, with the weight of Allied cavalry finally winning the day. But the French withdrew in order, flags flying and drums beating, after having inflicted terrible casualties on the Allies. The latter lost 21,000 killed and wounded, nearly twice the French losses.

When he first heard of Malplaquet, Louis assumed it was another disaster on the level of Blenheim, Ramillies, and Oudenarde. But when he received Villars's report, Louis realized that the Allies had gained only a Pyrrhic victory and that the French army remained intact. Villars assured Louis, 'If God gives us the grace to lose another similar battle, your Majesty can count on his enemies being destroyed.'

While Marlborough would never again fight a great battle, Malplaquet did not mark the end of his victories. In 1710 he captured further French fortresses in an attempt to break through Vauban's second line of the Pré Carré. Douai fell as did Béthune, St Venant, and Aire, but the frontier held. In 1711, Marlborough masterfully crossed the

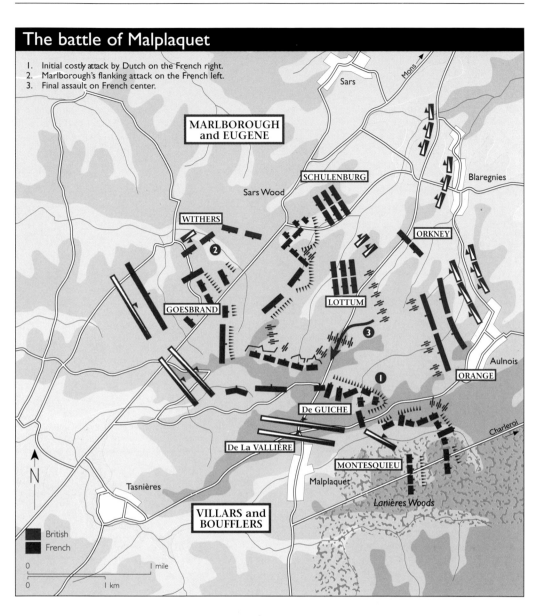

The battle of Malplaquet

1. Initial costly attack by Dutch on the French right.
2. Marlborough's flanking attack on the French left.
3. Final assault on French center.

Sars

Mons

MARLBOROUGH
and EUGENE

SCHULENBURG

Blaregnies

Sars Wood

WITHERS

ORKNEY

GOESBRAND

LOTTUM

Aulnois

ORANGE

De GUICHE

Charleroi

De La VALLIÈRE

MONTESQUIEU

Malplaquet

Tasnières

Lanières Woods

VILLARS and
BOUFFLERS

N

■ British
■ French

0   1 mile
0   1 km

last and most elaborate of the French
defensive lines, which the French had titled
the Ne Plus Ultra lines, and took Bouchain,
which capitulated on 12 September.
However, now he disappeared from Flanders.

The nature of the war changed in 1711.
Louis and Philip had already secured
irreversible victory in Spain by the close of
1710. Then, on 17 April 1711, Emperor
Joseph I died, leaving Archduke Charles heir
to the imperial crown and Habsburg lands.
Should the Allies succeed in putting him on
the throne of Spain, they would be creating a

monarchy more dangerous to the balance
of power in Europe than was a Spain ruled
by Philip V. This undermined the
determination of the alliance, and on
8 October the French and British concluded
the 'London Preliminaries,' by which
Louis pledged himself to recognize Anne
and the Protestant succession in Britain
and to ensure that the thrones of France
and Spain were never united.

FOLLOWING PAGES Battle of Malplaquet, 11
September 1709. (Roger-Viollet)

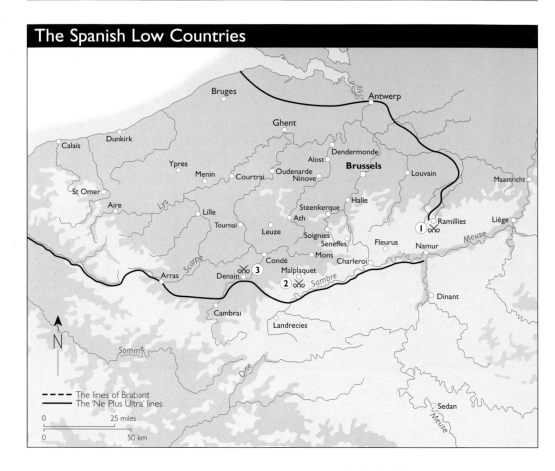

The Spanish Low Countries

1. Ramillies 23 May 1706
2. Malplaquet 11 September 1709
3. Denain 24 July 1712

Marlborough could not survive this new political climate. His wife Sarah, who had wielded considerable influence as a confidante of Queen Anne, had fallen from favor in 1710. Then in January 1712 Anne removed Marlborough from command. In May, she issued her 'Restraining Orders,' which instructed the new British commander, James Butler, Duke of Ormonde, to 'avoid engaging in any siege, or hazarding a battle, till you have further orders from Her Majesty.' On 16 July the French and British announced a suspension of arms.

Despite British defection, the fight continued. The majority of Ormonde's army was not British, but German units in British pay who quickly accepted Dutch money and leadership. The Habsburgs put Eugene in command of Allied forces in Flanders; however, Villars would get the better of him for the rest of the war. When Eugene invested Landrecies, Villars advanced to challenge the siege. On 24 July the French defeated elements of Eugene's forces at the Battle of Denain, although Eugene was not in personal command there. Villars invested Marchiennes, which fell on 30 July. French success at Denain and Marchiennes compelled Eugene to abandon the siege of Landrecies. Villars then took Douai, Le Quesnoy, and Bouchain in quick succession.

Soon the Treaties of Utrecht, concluded in April 1713 between France, Great Britain, the United Provinces, Savoy, Portugal, and Brandenburg-Prussia, ended the conflict between those adversaries. Only the Habsburgs remained unreconciled. During 1713 the fighting shifted to the Rhine, where Villars once again scored notable successes against Eugene, taking Landau and Freiburg.

The Treaty of Rastatt, on 7 March 1714, ended the war between Louis and Emperor Charles VI. By the treaties of Utrecht and Rastatt, Philip V was recognized as king of Spain by all save the Habsburgs, and Louis pledged that the crowns of Spain and France would never be united. England gained Gibraltar, Acadia, Hudson Bay, and Newfoundland. The Spanish Netherlands, Milan, Naples, and Sardinia passed to Austria and Savoy received Sicily.

The last fighting saw Philip V consolidate his control over Spanish territory. He finally retook Barcelona on 12 September 1714 and regained Minorca in June 1715. The wars of the Sun King had ended, and within a few months Louis himself would pass from this earth.

Marie Magdelaine Mouron

During the age of Louis XIV, illiteracy and a lack of interest in the lives of lesser folk conspired to confine rank-and-file soldiers to the shadows, where they remain anonymous to history. Lacking letters and memoirs, the historian must seek other sources to recapture details of life in the tents and the trenches. One such extraordinary document from 1696 records the interrogation of a deserter imprisoned in the fortress of St Omer. The officer in charge of hearing the case of this unfortunate individual was in a quandary and requested guidance from Paris. What so perplexed the officer was the nature of the deserter in question, because at a time when the army put only men in uniform, his prisoner had been revealed to be a woman.

Born Marie Magdelaine Mouron, she had grown up on the French coast near Boulogne. Her father first worked as a butcher and later bore arms, but not in a king's regiment. Rather, he served as a kind of armed guard and private soldier for the financiers who enforced and collected the salt tax, an important revenue for the Sun King. After Marie's mother died, her father remarried, but apparently the new wife turned out to be the wicked stepmother of legend. Not only was Marie's home life unhappy, but she had little hope for the future. A poor girl in her circumstances had few options; some menial employment – perhaps even prostitution – was all that awaited her. But Marie was a youth with a taste for adventure, and she decided that she could only break free of her destiny by assuming a man's identity.

There is no way of knowing for sure, but Marie may very well have heard the stories of women who had disguised their identities to serve as soldiers. Highly embellished tales of warrior women circulated in print: for example, the story of Geneviève Prémoy,

who was supposed to have taken the name of Chevalier Balthazar and performed so well under fire that Louis himself allowed her to maintain her rank even after her true sex became known. Beyond this, there was the fictionalized account of Christine de Meyrac, published as the *Héroïne mousquetaire*.

Probably sometime in 1690 – the record is not clear – Marie left home, slipped away to a nearby town, bought used men's clothing, discreetly changed into them, cropped her hair, and answered the recruiter's call. Her high voice and lack of facial hair could be explained as typical of an adolescent lad; perhaps 'he' was a bit underage and physically immature, but the expanding army needed troops, and so few questions would have been asked. Adopting the name 'Picard,' Marie signed on in a company commanded by Captain Destone of the Royal Walloon Regiment.

Marie soldiered as 'Picard' for a year and a half, ending up in the garrison at Sisteron, a fortress guarding the Durance river in Provence. There, as her interrogation reveals, she quarreled with another soldier and had to leave the army. The details are unclear, but she may have become unacceptable to the men of her unit, perhaps showing cowardice or perhaps being recognized as a woman. Even common soldiers at this time could approach an officer and ask that one of their fellows be banished from the regiment.

Be that as it may, from Sisteron she drifted to Avignon, where she once again enrolled, now as a dragoon in the Morsan Regiment. This time she took the name 'St Michel.' The fact that she was accepted as a dragoon suggests that Marie was a big girl, since dragoons put a premium on physical size. Her regiment saw service in Spain as part of the Duke de Noaille's small army in Catalonia.

From late May through mid-June 1693, the Morsan dragoons took part in the successful siege of the Catalonian port town of Rosas and its supporting fort of la Trinité. Marie's regiment anchored the extreme right flank of the French army. We have no account of Marie's actions during the siege, but she certainly took part in the foraging and skirmishing required of dragoons. While Noaille's campaign went well in Catalonia, the pressures against Louis's armies in Italy increased, and he had to dispatch five battalions to Marshal Catinat in Italy. This weakened Noaille's army to the point that it had to revert to the defensive, so after securing Rosas, he withdrew his army across the French border into Roussillon.

The Morsan dragoons quartered in Collioure; there 'St Michel' became embroiled with another dragoon named St Jean, and the dispute led to a duel. In the fight, she received a sword cut so deep that she was unable to stop the flow of blood and had to seek medical attention, thus revealing her sex to the regimental surgeon.

As luck would have it, this was the day when Marshal Noailles was to review the regiment. Marie, once more openly a woman, pleaded with the Marshal, telling him of her adventures, and he took pity on her, giving her to the care of the wife of an artillery officer. Noailles also arranged that upon her recovery Marie would go to be schooled, or 'instructed,' in Perpignan. However, Marie did not fit in. By now she was as much a dragoon as a young woman, and mistreatment at the hand of the headmistress drove Marie to rebel. In one final dispute, Marie heaved a plate of salad at the headmistress's head and ran away.

She now undertook an epic journey on foot. By modern roads, the distance from Perpignan to St Omer is about 680 miles (1,100 km), but Marie's travels along country paths must have been much longer. The first stage of her trek took her only as far as Montpellier, where she became so desperately ill that she had to remain in a hospital for several months, during which time she was bled 13 or 14 times, by her

account. Eventually she reached St Omer, but the record is mute on how long it took her and on how she supported herself along the road. It is clear, however, that at least two and a half years passed between the time of her duel and her return to the ranks in 1696.

The final drama came when she once again enlisted, now as 'La Garenne,' in the company of Desbrière of the du Biez infantry regiment in March 1696. She appears to have taken a recruitment bounty at this time, the usual reward for enlisting. She was obviously taken with the military life, but the clock was running out on her. By now Marie had spent at least five years in the army and on the road, and sun and toil had undoubtedly weathered her face. It must have been increasingly hard for her to convince others that she was a beardless adolescent lad. Her fellows in the Desbrière company began to remark publicly that 'La Garenne' must really be a woman.

'La Garenne' began to pass 'his' off-duty hours with two other soldiers from her company, Langenois and Languedoc, who planned to desert. Marie testified later that she tried to dissuade them but failed. Her knowledge of their intentions, she said, convinced her to flee lest she be punished because of her close association with Langenois and Languedoc. She slipped away from the regiment by herself on 1 May.

Hiding her coat and stockings, which would give her away as a soldier, she walked the 12 miles (20 km) to Aire and tried to enlist in the Sanzé Regiment. The lieutenant-colonel of the regiment, La Bussière, into whose company Marie tried to enroll, challenged her, doubting that she was a man. At this point Marie broke down and admitted that she was a woman, but it did not stop there. La Bussière recognized the vest she wore as uniform issue in the du Biez Regiment, and she further admitted that she was a deserter. La Bussière arrested her.

What were her sins? The most obvious charge could have been sexual misconduct; prostitutes, when apprehended, received harsh treatment. However, there was no evidence that Marie was guilty of liaisons with men, or women for that matter. When a woman jailer inspected Marie to ensure that she was a woman, she also probably confirmed Marie's virginity, for the court accepted her statement on oath that she had never had sexual relations with any man. With her propriety established, the simple fact that she was a woman in the ranks would have led only to her dismissal.

Her captain, Desbrière, maintained charges against her less because he had lost a soldier than because he had been robbed of an investment. Marie had certainly received a recruitment bounty, and Desbrière stated that she received pay for March and April –

Marshal Catinat, who gained great victories in Italy, differed from Louis's other marshals in that he did not come from an exalted family of the military aristocracy, but from humbler origins in the recently ennobled administrative and legal class. (AKG, Berlin)

money gone to no purpose now. In addition, he would be out for any uniform items or equipment she took with her, since it was the captain's responsibility to replace these in the case of desertion. Making it all worse, in trying to enroll in another regiment, she would have accepted another bounty. Thus she was a *rôleur*, someone who went, or 'rolled,' from one regiment to another to pocket several bounties.

The penalty inflicted on male deserters was draconic – branding the cheek, cutting the nose and ears, and condemnation to service on the king's galleys for life. It was recognized from the start that this was not on the cards for Marie, that she would face only incarceration. While her fate is uncertain, an undecipherable scrawl in the margins of her file seems to direct that she be committed to prison for a long term.

Beyond its novelty, this story provides a good deal of information on life in the ranks. Marie's life demonstrates that a woman could bear up to the toils and duties of military life in the 17th century. More profoundly, it speaks of the proximity but privacy of military life. Men lived in close confines; when quartered they regularly slept two to a bed, but they did not disrobe. Marie's interrogation reported that 'although she has almost always slept with some comrade,' she 'always did it so well that she had never been recognized for what she was.'

Obviously Marie did not disrobe or bathe with her fellows, and this fact was not regarded as so unusual as to draw notice. Urination clearly posed certain issues. One reason why it seems necessary that she had heard of other women soldiers before becoming one herself is that she must have figured out how to urinate standing up. We know from other accounts that this could be done by using a bored-out animal horn or a metal tube; some device must have been part of her kit from the first day. The fact that she was recognized as a deserter because of her clothing tells us that in the French army uniforms had become common by the 1690s. Her disputes, one ending in a duel, imply a sense of honor among the rank and file that mimicked that among officers.

But perhaps the most important fact that we learn from Marie's career under arms is the mobility enjoyed by the troops. At a time when a peasant might never travel more than a few miles from his place of birth, Marie marched from the English Channel to the Mediterranean, from Provence to Catalonia. Today, the military is associated with patriotic sentiment; however, Marie lived in a time when parochialism, not nationalism, was the rule. The fact that hundreds of thousands of individuals left their homes and visited the length and breadth of France helped to create a sense of the land and people of France. The much-expanded armies of the 17th century not only defended the state but helped to create a sense of nationhood.

Predatory armies

From a distance of several centuries, the armies of Louis XIV might seem lethargic, fighting few battles and prone to stately sieges. However, these forces were constantly active, forever on the prowl, for they were great predatory beasts. Despite the efforts of military administrators to amass magazines of war matériel, particularly grain, armies of this period had to draw much of what they needed from villages and towns within their reach. Armies' needs to supply themselves within the war zone could make the lives of civilians there a tragedy of violence, loss, and suffering.

Armies drew fodder, food, and funds from the hapless populations that lay in the path of war. The search for fodder alone required an endless succession of petty operations by war parties. No army could carry with it enough sustenance for its horses, which could each consume 55 lb (25 kg) of green forage per day. Hauling such a weight of fodder would have been impossible. Instead, armies sent out armed forage parties that numbered in the thousands of men to harvest grasslands systematically, denying peasants needed pasturage. Then, having denuded an area of forage, armies changed camp to find virgin fields. Armies and fortresses dispatched detachments to seek food for the troops, seizing grain to be baked into bread or returning to camp with herds of cattle and sheep in tow. Raids garnered rations.

Armies also helped to finance war by imposing contributions, sending out armed parties to impose and collect cash payments to fill the army's coffers. Soldiers punished refusal to surrender the sum demanded by carrying out 'execution,' which meant the burning of farms, villages, and towns to chastise the recalcitrant and 'encourage' compliance by others. In border conflicts, rival armies might each make demands on the other's home territory, in which case one side or both might try to dissuade his foe from torching villages by resorting to reprisals. During the War of Reunions, French officials threatened the most brutal reprisals. In a particularly vicious instruction from the War of the Reunions, Louis ordered Marshal Humières 'always to burn fifty [enemy] houses or villages for every one which will have been burned on my lands.'

To draw their sustenance from the surrounding population, predatory armies had to cull the herd, not eliminate it. Armies that were too rapacious drove the peasants out of the countryside, and as Villars commented to Louis in 1703, 'where there are no peasants there are no supplies.' This same commander warned his own troops in 1707, as he led them across the Rhine: 'My friends … If you burn, if you make the people run away, you will die of hunger.'

Even the quartering of troops impinged on the lives of civilians. While on campaign, armies camped together in the field under canvas. However, when the army went into quarters for the winter, and in Spain at mid-summer, the troops dispersed into civilian homes, most commonly in towns. Friendly populations who housed troops were supposed to receive compensation, while neutral and hostile areas were required to take in troops as another form of war tax. Soldiers were nearly always unwanted guests, and exemptions from quartering troops were much prized by those, such as nobles and crown officials, who possessed them. Boarded soldiers might abuse families, defile women, and demand additional payments.

Because armies depended so much on local resources, one way to deny an area to an enemy was to strip the countryside of everything that a foe might need. This legitimated the most brutal devastation. War parties were often told to take what they needed and could carry, while destroying the rest. Many a barn went up in flames to deny the enemy the fodder kept within. Larger units might be dispatched to 'eat up the countryside,' leaving nothing for the enemy. In fact, the worst violence towards people and goods came not in securing resources for oneself, but in denying them to the enemy. An army living off the country wished to preserve the sources of supply; an army hoping to create a desert to hamper a foe had no interest in sparing fields, stores, or people.

The most extreme case of a strategy of destruction came with the devastation of the Palatinate in 1688–89. Earlier, in 1674, Turenne had tried to make it difficult if not impossible for the enemy to maintain himself. In order to protect the northern flank of Alsace and the fortress of Philippsburg, Turenne ravaged the country. 'Nothing in the world,' he claimed, 'is so key to hindering a siege of Philippsburg than to have foraged all the places where the enemy could assemble to sustain himself.' The decimation ordered by Turenne was bad enough, but that in 1688–89 was far greater. When Louis's initial gambit to bring the Germans to terms in 1688 failed, he accepted a policy of defending his frontier by turning the lands immediately to the north and east of Alsace into a wasteland incapable of sustaining an enemy army. This would be the most systematic destruction.

As early as October, the King's advisors considered a policy of demolishing German towns. After the fall of Mannheim on 15 November, Louvois wrote:

I see the King is rather disposed to entirely raze the city and citadel of Mannheim, and, in this case, to utterly destroy the houses, in such a manner that no stone stands on another.

Should such destruction befall Mannheim, the enemy could neither employ that town as a base of operations nor quarter troops there. A month later, Louvois instructed a local commander, Montclair:

His Majesty recommends to you to completely ruin [faire bien ruiner] all the places that you leave along the lower and upper Neckar so that the enemy, finding no forage or food whatever, will not try to approach there.

Louvois drafted a list of towns to be destroyed, and in late December 1688 and January 1689 he dispatched a series of letters urging a faster pace of demolition in a campaign that peaked from March through early June. Troops commanded by Tessé, then a subordinate of Montclair, drove the inhabitants of Heidelberg from their homes and torched the town on 2 March. However, perhaps warned of the French plans, the townspeople had prepared for this eventuality, quickly returned to their homes, and fought the fires as the French marched out. As a result, instead of several hundred houses being consumed by fire, the flames devoured only 30–35 dwellings.

But if Heidelberg escaped the worst, Mannheim did not. On 13 January 1689, Louvois ordered the destruction of that town, informing Montclair:

The King wants that the inhabitants of Mannheim be warned to withdraw to Alsace, and that all the buildings of the city be razed, without leaving any structure standing.

The devil's work was not done until early March. Montclair informed the local magistrates on 4 March that the French intended to utterly demolish the town, and suggested that the townspeople rip down their own dwellings 'to avoid disorder'; not surprisingly, they refused to do so. In accord with Louis's desire that the good people of Mannheim relocate to Alsace, where they could become his loyal subjects, the French ordered the inhabitants of Mannheim to pack their belongings and leave. Yet the French allowed so little time that the unfortunate inhabitants were allowed to put their goods in churches until transport was arranged.

The torches began to burn the town on 8 March and continued over the next few days. Flames promised to do a through job,

as Montclair explained: 'Since the town is
almost all built of wood, it will soon be
consumed.' Troops completed the
destruction by ripping down town walls and
filling in ditches; to speed the effort, the
authorities conscripted peasants as forced
labor. After the townspeople had evacuated,
Louvois instructed Montclair to shoot any
who tried to return to their homes. Chamlay
could report that Mannheim had been
leveled, 'like a field.'

A score of other substantial towns shared
Mannheim's fate – Speyer, Worms,
Oppenheim, and Bingen among them. Duras
informed Louvois that among the smoking
ruins of Worms, no house remained
standing. In addition to the destruction of
major towns, the French burnt a great many
surrounding villages to the ground. Tessé
stated that French troops had torched all the
villages within 4 leagues (19 km) of
Mannheim.

As the French set fire to elegant houses
and modest cottages, their formal orders
were to act in a disciplined manner, but it
was hard to avoid outright pillage. Troops
ordered to burn saw little point in not
stealing the goods in the house; after all, it
was all to be put to the torch anyway. Should
occupants resist, marauders abused or killed
them. Raiding parties operating beyond the
eyes of senior officers had little reason to
restrain themselves. The behavior of different
parties inevitably must have varied,
depending on the individuals who
comprised them, but at worst they would
not have respected orders or decency. The
fact that many filled their bellies with wine
from the cellars of homes slated for
destruction could only have exaggerated the
tendency for troops to get out of control.

As is so often the case in warfare, excess
bred retaliation, and the hard-put German
peasantry took up arms against the French.
In doing so, they followed a strong
17th-century precedent. In engravings from
the 1630s, *Les misères et les maleurs de la
guerre*, the artist Jacques Callot fashioned a
memorable record of violence against and by
the peasantry in war. One of the best-known

This engraving by Jacques Callot, 'Pillaging of a Large
Farm House,' brutally displays the barbarity of marauding
troops during the Thirty Years' War. Soldiers torture men
to make them reveal where they have hidden their
valuables as others steal, kill, and rape. (AKG, Berlin)

images in this series portrays the pillage of a
farmhouse, as soldiers murder, torture, and
rape. This violent image is followed by a
depiction of peasants' revenge, with the
caption:

*After the soldiers have committed much
devastation, finally the peasants, whom they
have treated as enemies, await them in a
secluded place and by surprise ... put them to
death.*

Armed largely with the tools of
agricultural labor, peasants smash skulls with
grain-flails and skewer the guilty with
pitchforks.

In 1674 Turenne's troops encountered
armed resistance from the population of the
Rhineland. These resentful peasants wielded
more than grain-flails. Armed with muskets
and acting as snipers, the *schnapphans* picked

off French raiders from cover. The term *schnapphans* literally meant 'highwaymen,' but in this circumstance it referred to peasants who made life miserable for the marauding troops. When the French found their own men mutilated, they responded with greater cruelty of their own.

With the later devastation of the Palatinate, the *schnapphans* once again cut down the French. General Huxelles reported back to Louvois in March 1689, 'all the peasants are armed and on their guard.' Huxelles went on to report that he had tried to disarm the peasantry but had to admit:

I believe that it is difficult to take arms away in such a manner that there do not remain enough [for the peasants] to put themselves in the woods and disturb those who pass as soon as the leaves come out.

Raiding parties and convoys, by land and by river, fell victim to *schnapphans*, whose 'numbers were swelled by the peasants of the Palatinate who desert every day.' Goupillières went on to testify that the islands of the Rhine were swarming with these snipers. Chamlay complained that they:

fire from all the woods and all the passages. It is absolutely necessary to bring these people back to reason by taking them [prisoner] and by burning their villages.

Schnapphans were all the more beyond the pale because they did not take prisoners.

The nature of logistics and war finance, both of which saw armies search for their own resources in the field, lent the world of war a level of violence directed toward civilian populations that continued some of the extremes of the Thirty Years' War and cruelly foreshadowed the victimization of civilian populations that so typified warfare in the 20th century.

Mme. De Sévigné

The letters of Marie de Rabutin-Chantal, Marquise de Sévigné (1626–96), come down to us as one of the great literary records of aristocratic life in 17th-century France. As an observer of the world around her, she was not so distracted by the brilliance of the Sun King that she could not see the harder, and darker, aspects of existence. Among the repertoire of her commentaries, she wrote strong words on honor, war, and rebellion.

Born in 1626 to a father who traced his ancestry back to old Burgundian nobility and a mother whose family had risen into the aristocracy through finance, Marie de Rabutin-Chantal was orphaned at the age of six. Nonetheless, growing up in the household of her uncle, she enjoyed what she described as an idyllic childhood – 'Never a youth so halcyon as mine!' Possessed of high intelligence, she received an excellent education. A pretty woman with a sizeable dowry, she attracted Henri de Sévigné, a Breton noble, and married in 1644.

Henri was a dashing rogue who fathered two children with his young wife – Françoise Marguerite (b. 1646) and Charles (b. 1648) – but left her little else at his death. He squandered her wealth and pursued mistresses with the flourish expected in that swashbuckling age. Among those who received his attentions was the famous (or infamous) Ninon, perhaps the most renowned courtesan of Paris. Dismissed by Ninon, he had gone on to a more questionable woman, 'La Belle Lolo.' Before long, another gallant, Chevalier d'Albret, challenged Sévigné over the lady's favors, and in the resulting duel d'Albret's blade pierced Sévigné's heart, and his young wife became a widow in 1651.

Mme. de Sévigné spent the next two decades immersed in Parisian society, managing her Breton lands, and raising her children. She never remarried, although she certainly had suitors, probably including Fouquet, the finance minister under Mazarin. After being exploited by one man, she resolved to retain her independence; a wife was ruled by her husband, but a widow managed her own affairs.

With the years, Mme. de Sévigné focused on, some would say obsessed over, her daughter, whom she called 'the prettiest girl in France.' This daughter married well in 1669, to Count Grignan. At first the young couple set up in Paris, but by the end of the year Louis XIV had appointed Count Grignan as lieutenant-governor of Provence, the king's viceroy in that important southern province. Soon Mme. de Sévigné's daughter had to take up residence in Grignan, the family estate in Provence, so hundreds of miles separated mother from beloved daughter, and Mme. de Sévigné crossed this gap with a bridge of letters.

Most of the observations and commentaries offered by Mme. de Sévigné concerned court life, gossip, and the details of her own existence; however, from time to time she discussed military values, the army, and war. After all, as a woman of the well-placed nobility, she was surrounded by soldiers and talk of fighting.

The military participation of her family exemplifies the upper reaches of the aristocracy. Mme. de Sévigné dismissed the infantry as 'the workhouse,' implying that it was led by impoverished or ill-born officers. Count Grignan, her son-in-law, commanded a cavalry regiment. Her own son, Charles, a man of limited success, opted for a military career, and in 1669 she bought him a commission as ensign in the highly prestigious elite cavalry company Gendarmes-Dauphin for the princely sum of 75,000 *livres*. He played his part well in the Dutch War, receiving public praise for his bravery at Seneffe, where he took a slight wound. Mme. de Sévigné's letters show a mother's concern for the safety of her son, but pride in his courage. Charles purchased a second lieutenant's commission and once again proved his bravery in 1678 at the battle of St Denis. Reporting her son's performance, she wrote: 'having escaped death ten or twelve times near Mons – he should live forever.'

Two years later, however, Charles distressed his mother by announcing that he wanted to sell his commission. She commented that this would bring the end of his possibilities at court. 'The King cannot abide those who leave the service.' The unhappy Charles finally sold his commission at a substantial loss, but he continued to bear arms for the king in the next war as colonel of aristocratic militia, a force not really on a par with the regular army. Mme. de Sévigné clearly was not happy with her son's career, feeling that her money had been poorly invested.

Her grandson, Louis-Provence, Marquis de Grignan (1671–1704), was a far more distinguished soldier. He entered the service as the kind of child officer typical of the highly privileged; at age 16 the lad commanded a company of cavalry. Wounded in the leg by a shell at the siege of Mannheim in 1688, he caught the king's eye. When he had recovered from his injuries, he bought his uncle's cavalry regiment, becoming a colonel at age 18, not an unusual phenomenon for top nobles. Mme. de Sévigné was always very solicitous concerning 'the little colonel.' The Marquis continued to rise after the death of his grandmother. He distinguished himself at the Battle of Blenheim in 1704, but died later that year from smallpox.

So close to men in the army, Mme. de Sévigné mused about values that inspired them. In one of her most interesting interchanges, she discussed the nature of that most central aristocratic virtue of the 17th century – the pursuit of gloire. A friend of hers, Cardinal de Retz, had written, 'That which makes men truly great and raises them above the rest of the world is the love

of la belle gloire.' For all that she paid the price of masculine gloire, Mme. de Sévigné accepted and even promoted the concept. She regarded it as an important part of male education:

Since one constantly tells men that they are only worthy of esteem to the extent that they love gloire, they devote all their thoughts to it; and this shapes all French bravery.

She contrasted masculine virtue with feminine vice: 'As women are allowed to be weak, they take advantage of this privilege without scruple.' Her cousin and frequent correspondent, Count de Bussy-Rabutin, responded to her observations:

You are weak, Madame, because you have been taught to be so. If you had been raised with the thought that your honor consisted in killing men, instead of in the idea only of loving them, I assure you that you would have been as brave as an Amazon.

Male concepts of personal gloire fostered aggression, and grieved their womenfolk, but, as evidenced by Mme. de Sévigné, women raised their sons in this tradition. Of course, the desire for gloire goes a long way to explain not only the conduct of officers, but the policy of Louis XIV as well.

The worship of gloire required blood sacrifice, and the French aristocracy boasted that it paid a 'tax in blood.' Those impositions could be heavy. Mme de Sévigné reported on the arrival of casualty lists at court. The costly and indecisive battle of Seneffe in August 1674 brought a huge butcher's bill. She wrote:

We have lost so much by this victory that without the Te Deum and some [captured] flags brought to Notre Dame, we would believe we had lost the battle.

Mme. de Sévigné reported more triumphantly in 1690, after the battles of Fleurus and Beachy Head, 'There are Te Deums for the victories on land, and others

This portrait of the remarkable Mme. de Sévigné, painted by Lefebvre c. 1665, hangs in a house she once occupied in Paris, now the Musée Carnavalet. (Ann Ronan Picture Library)

of the victories at sea.' However, such success came at a price, and the casualty list from Fleurus inspired some of her most surprising prose. Tallies of the fallen gave the names of the officers, but only totals for the rank and file, an ultimate comment on their anonymity. Seeing the roll call of aristocratic officers killed, Mme de Sévigné commented to Count de Bussy-Rabutin:

I have only general pity for all these who have perished in this battle … I pity as well their poor mothers, like Mme de Saucourt and Mme de Cauvisson. But as for the young widows, they are hardly to be pitied, for they will be happy to be their own mistresses or to change masters.

This seemingly hard-hearted comment obviously grew out of her own experience; she was far happier as a widow than she had been as a wife. A duel delivered her independence; battle had now done the same for 'the young widows.'

Her usual comments on the clash of arms were made from afar; she was at court, not at the front. However, when tax revolt broke out in Brittany, she was at Les Rochers, her estate in that province. The costs of the Dutch War drove up the impositions exacted by the monarchy, one of which involved a stamp tax. Only specially stamped paper could be used for certain legal documents, forcing people to buy the extremely expensive stamped paper, or *papier timbré*; this amounted to a stiff tax on legal transactions.

In 1675, tax rebellions, generically known as the Papier Timbré revolts, hit a number of towns in western France, including Le Mans, Poitiers, Agen, and Bordeaux. Disturbances also broke out in Rennes, the traditional capital of Brittany, in April. After this, acts of resistance spread to the countryside of Brittany, where the rebels were know as Bonnets Rouges because of the red caps worn by the peasants. The violence frightened Mme. de Sévigné, who wrote in July: 'These demons have come to pillage and burn right up to Fougères; that is a little too close to Les Rochers.' Against the advice of the Duke de Chaulnes, governor of Brittany and a friend of Mme. de Sévigné, Louis dispatched troops to punish the rebellious province even after the troubles had subsided.

Mme. de Sévigné offered lurid reports of brutal repression by the king's soldiers. She announced that Chaulnes would bring 4,000 troops to punish Rennes and that 'It is believed that there will be a lot of hanging.' Soon she reported that the authorities had seized 'twenty-five or thirty men that were going to be hanged.' She concluded, 'this province is a good example for the other, and especially to respect the governors and their wives.' She had been scandalized when crowds threw stones at Chaulnes's residence, and she obviously feared attacks on her son-in-law and daughter.

As the repression continued, Mme. de Sévigné became more callous toward the rebels. 'We are no longer breaking so many on the wheel – one in eight days, only to maintain justice.' The stories became more

grisly as 10,000 troops were quartered on the countryside, where they persecuted the locals. 'As for our soldiers,' she wrote to her daughter in January 1676, 'they amuse themselves by stealing, and the other day put a baby (*petit enfant*) on a spit.'

Mme. de Sévigné died not in Brittany, or in Paris, which she loved, but in Provence while staying with her daughter at Grignan on 17 April 1696. She had led a life perfectly placed to observe the young Louis XIV mature and establish his *gloire* through the pursuit of war.

This tapestry depicting Marlborough at the battle of Blenheim is one of several tapestries decorating Blenheim Palace, the grand home awarded to Marlborough by a grateful government. (Ann Ronan Picture Library)

Peace by exhaustion

Attrition ultimately imposed accommodation and peace on the adversaries at the end of each major war fought by the Sun King. His minor struggles – the War of Devolution and the War of the Reunions – did not follow this pattern; both lasted for about a year, not enough time to exhaust the resources of France. Louis came out ahead in the treaties that ended these two brief clashes, but each peace left him only partially satisfied. As a result of his unresolved desires, the lesser wars served as preludes to more cataclysmic confrontations that followed. Therefore, the focus must shift to Louis's great wars, which followed the pattern of war-as-process.

From a diplomatic point of view, Louis regained peace in each of these contests by first detaching one key member from the opposing coalitions, and thereby breaking them up. The cracks in the alliances soon penetrated them and split them open. The Dutch War spun down very quickly after Louis, in June 1678, won over the Dutch to the principle of concluding a separate peace with France. The formal treaty followed in August, and the other parties agreed to end the war in succession; Spain signed the next month, and the emperor in February 1679. An agreement with the duke of Savoy provided the key to ending the Nine Years' War. Louis reached some understanding with Victor Amadeus in 1695, making that year's campaign a staged affair, and, after the Sun King finally agreed to meet Victor Amadeus's demands in the early months of 1696, the two concluded a foramal treaty in August 1696. The rest of the alliance accepted peace a year later, in September and October of 1697.

England proved to be the linchpin of the alliance against Louis in the War of the Spanish Succession. The changing fate of the Austrian Habsburgs, with the death of Joseph I in 1711 elevating Archduke Charles to the imperial throne, changed everything, because winning Charles the Spanish throne as well would now create a Habsburg superstate. This sapped much of the logic behind British policy, and Louis was able to detach Queen Anne from the alliance by 1712. Charles VI may not have been happy to abandon his designs on the Spanish throne, but British defection brought the other major contestants to sign a peace treaty in 1713, and Charles had to follow suit in 1714.

Of course, to say that one breaks a hostile alliance by first separating off and reconciling with one of its members may not be saying much. The disintegration of an alliance must start somewhere; it would be odd if it collapsed all at once. But the important thing about Louis's ability to cut out a member of an alliance was that he did so by diplomatic compromise, not military compulsion.

This is not to deny military action any share in ending wars, but it operated more to make victory seem impossible than to award it to either side. The fact that Louis could not, in fact, occupy the Dutch Netherlands, as proven by 1674, and that the Dutch and Spanish could not drive him from the Spanish Netherlands assured a compromise peace. Louis gave up hopes of taking the Spanish Netherlands as a whole, but the Allies conceded Franche-Comté and critical Flanders fortresses to France. The Sun King's considerable success on campaign during the Nine Years' War prepared the way for a conclusion to the war by making it clear that his enemies could not defeat him. The concluding treaties won him no new gains – in fact he lost certain of the Reunions, most notably Luxembourg – but the terms did guarantee his frontiers.

Even at the darkest hours of the War of the Spanish Succession, Louis's forces did well enough on one front or another to stave off defeat. Campaign success came closest to dictating the final solution in Spain itself, where Franco–Spanish forces did finally *win* the war. However, looking at the war overall, the most important conclusion was negative: that even the brilliant successes of Marlborough could not dictate a peace.

In lieu of a military decision, wars continued until the pressure of attrition, and evolving circumstances, made the contending parties ready to accept a compromise peace. One adversary survived and in surviving tried to increase the costs his enemy had to pay. This affected operations considerably, particularly the pressure to make war feed war. Adversaries jockeyed for position on the battlefield and around the conference table, while the burdens of war increased and made parties more willing to accept terms. In this process, troubles at home resulting from declining trade, rising taxes, and internal dissent balanced against prospects for territorial gain, commercial benefits, and matters of principle. Diplomatic maneuvering should not be seen outside the context of war and the costs of war, but neither should the conduct of campaigns be regarded as the soul determinant of the wars of the Sun King. It was more complicated than that.

The legacies of war

As is virtually always true of great historical events, the consequences of the wars of the Sun King are both obvious and elusive, sure and debatable. The change of territory is as clear as a line on a map; the impact on society, beyond the loss of people and property, is more subtle and questionable.

The negatives of war are easiest to establish. Louis's major conflicts were wars of attrition, implying great cost to the peoples who fought them. It is impossible to calculate the toll of casualties with any certainty. Jack Levy has estimated the battle deaths alone during Louis's three main wars as exceeding 2,250,000, which seems high; this, of course, includes casualties among all adversaries over several decades. Deaths related to war but not due to combat could easily exceed the numbers lost in actual fighting. Famines of 1693–94 and 1709–10 drive the totals even higher, although to put it as an exact figure exceeds our knowledge. 'Millions' must suffice.

Beyond the losses, there are other negatives to consider – what the wars did not accomplish. They did not save Europe from a French attempt to conquer the continent; Louis was too concerned with legitimacy, too much of a traditionalist, to attempt a Napoleonic expansion. Louis sought preeminence for himself and France in Europe, but ultimately he had no intention of absorbing it. His goals stayed within his interpretation of his just claims, based on dynasty and history. That interpretation was self-serving but not limitless.

Also, the wars of the Sun King did not spell the end for any state. Louis came closest to doing so when he seized Lorraine from its duke in 1670 and relinquished it only in 1697. He had offered to restore it to the Duke in 1678, but the latter could not accept French terms. Emperor Joseph I did seize the duchy of Mantua in 1707 as retaliation for the duke's support of Louis in Italy, and William III did lose Orange to France, but these were secondary or tertiary affairs. Louis might have fundamentally reduced the United Provinces had he taken Amsterdam in 1672–73. His rejection of generous terms in 1672 suggests that Louis would have countenanced an even further reduction of Dutch land and power, but it did not come to pass. Certainly Spain changed dynasties, but that change resulted from the natural death of Charles II and the highly legitimate claims of Louis's progeny to inherit the Spanish throne. It has been argued that the Glorious Revolution in England came as a result of Louis's wars, but it had much more to do with English dynastic circumstances, religious convictions, and internal politics than with threats from France.

The power of great states certainly changed during the wars of the Sun King. England – Great Britain after 1707 – certainly rose to unrivaled naval supremacy. It ruled the waves more by commitment than by combat, for the British were willing and able to make a huge investment in their fleet. As Britain rose, the United Provinces declined to second- or third-rate status. Under William III the Dutch were the center of gravity of the anti-French coalition, but by the end of the War of the Spanish Succession, Britain had taken the lead.

In Germany, Habsburg Austria reclaimed great-power status. At the start of Louis's personal reign, these Habsburgs were still reeling from the effects of the Thirty Years' War, but the events of the 1680s increased their power dramatically. Yet Vienna grew stronger not by fighting France, but by conquering lands ruled by the Ottoman Turks. Brandenberg–Prussia became a significant power, from its low point during the Thirty Years' War, but it would only claim major status with Frederick the Great after 1740. The Russia of Peter the Great battled its way to prominence during the Great Northern War (1700–21); however, this conflict was outside Louis's orbit, a coincident but entirely separate struggle.

Above all, the relative power of France decreased as a consequence of Louis's wars. Under the Sun King, France enjoyed a kind of hegemony in Europe but would not do so again until Napoleon. French resources and population were too great for France to fall below the level of a great power, but after 1714 it was simply one among several. In a sense, the Bourbon monarchy never recovered from the costs of Louis's wars.

Yet there is no denying the territorial gains secured by the Sun King. At a time when he reigned but did not rule, the Treaties of Westphalia gave France complicated but effective control of Alsace in 1648. The Treaty of the Pyrenees, Mazarin's work, added most of Artois and small portions of Flanders, Hainault, and Luxembourg to France, while along the Pyrenees border, Louis gained the county of Rousillon and part of Cerdagne. During his personal reign, Louis added the entire province of Franche–Comté, parts of Flanders, Artois, and Hainaut on his north-east frontier, and Orange and a small addition to Dauphiné in the south. He also held Lorraine for a time, but not permanently.

A comparison with Napoleon is inevitable and illuminating. Napoleon, the archetypal conqueror whose military genius still commands the attention of soldiers today, actually left France much smaller in 1814 and 1815 than he found it when he seized power in 1799, since revolutionary France had absorbed the Austrian Netherlands and other borderlands. He ultimately lost territory and his throne, to die a prisoner on St Helena. In contrast, Louis, who also took on a European coalition, added to the domain and population of France, secured another kingdom for his dynasty, and died in bed at Versailles.

Louis's war-as-process achieved lasting gains; Napoleon's war-as-event achieved great battlefield triumphs but ended by

diminishing France, and at a terrible cost. Part of the explanation for the permanence of Louis's conquests may be that wars ended by long negotiations and compromise after enervating struggles may have left contending parties satisfied and tired enough that they were unwilling to challenge the results in later clashes. However, more fundamental was the fact that Louis operated within the international system of his day, respecting its methods and moderation. In contrast, Napoleon overthrew the international system and its restraints. In the short run, Napoleon dumbfounded his enemies, isolated them, and had his way. In the long run, they recognized the threat he posed, and because that threat was so great, they banded together so that their combined force might defeated him.

Wars shaped not only the boundaries of states, but also the institutions of government within those frontiers. Here it is easiest to focus on France. Historians still debate the extent to which the wars of the Sun King fostered the growth in France of a strong, centralized, bureaucratic monarchy – what is traditionally referred to as 'absolutism.' Some interested in society argue that Louis did not transform class relationships; others concerned with local authority insist that Louis did not really concentrate power at the center. However, to look at Louis's army is to see absolutism, for he asserted royal authority there as it had never been imposed before. Also, the army was the largest institution of the state. In achieving this, Louis harnessed and humbled his aristocracy, at least in their military roles. To look at the conduct of international relations also reveals the King in control. Central bureaucracy, at least as it dealt with the demands of war, unquestionably expanded in size and authority. Absolutism in the sense of a king all-powerful in all things may have not existed, but the Bourbon monarchy did assume and exercise greater power during the wars of Louis XIV.

Perhaps Louis's most fatal shortcoming concerned state finance, and his failure here had the greatest consequence. Louis's wars literally bankrupted the state, although a formal consideration and revocation of debt would not take place until 1716. The ruin of state finances and the impoverishment of the common people to enrich the gods of war were bad enough, but the way in which the Bourbon monarchy dealt with its debt had very important implications for the 18th century.

Louis was never able to overcome his need for short-term credit at high interest. His transcendent concern to control something as crucial as state finance made it impossible for him to delegate this matter to the financial and commercial communities that supplied the money, as was the case in England and the United Provinces. These two rivals boasted the great Bank of Amsterdam (1609) and the Bank of England (1694), which created reliable and stable money markets that channeled loans to the state at low interest. Those who loaned money through the banks were also in charge of the state purse strings, and they could be sure to repey themselves without default. Such security justified relatively cheap loans. But Louis paid top dollar for loans, and this increased state debt to unmanageable levels. Partial bankruptcy could alleviate the worst for a while, but ultimately it just made things worse. Louis never solved the problem of war finance, and so he bequeathed this problem to his successors.

The implications of Louis's fiscal policy for the future loom even greater when one takes into calculation the fact that he tried to raise unprecedented amounts of money to fund war without challenging the fiscal privileges of the aristocracy and the Church. Nobles retained their tax breaks, particularly their full or partial exemption from the *taille* (land and property tax) and the *gabelle* (salt tax stemming from the government monopoly). He did create two modest new taxes designed to tap the wealth of all classes: first, the *capitation*, or head tax,

in 1695, which was revived in 1701, and second, the *dixième* in 1710. Such taxes were also supposed to hit everyone, but the Church bought itself off both the *capitation* and the *dixième*, while the nobility paid, but not in proportion to its wealth.

Interestingly, Vauban, that highly energetic and fertile mind, proposed a thorough overhaul of taxation to produce an equitable system without aristocratic exemptions – his *dîme royale* – at the end of his life, but lost royal favor because of it. By not confronting this essential issue, Louis passed on a system of privilege that would ultimately undermine the monarchy. The Sun King failed to employ his great prestige and power to attack tax privilege; the self-indulgent Louis XV would not confront this issue, and the weak Louis XVI only faced it when it was too late.

Louis may have founded a kind of absolutism because of and through the demands of war, but the way he turned to fiscal expedients instead of reform may have doomed the Bourbons. When the Estates General met in 1789, precipitating the French Revolution, it did so to deal with a financial crisis that had its immediate roots in the War of American Independence, but which stretched back much further. Louis may have increased French domains and won a new throne for his dynasty, but it is not stretching things beyond credibility to say that he might also have condemned them to revolution. If this is true, the impact of the wars of the Sun King were profound indeed.

Louis did not live long after the end of his last war; he died on 1 September 1715. On his deathbed, Louis XIV is reported to have admitted to the boy of five who would succeed him, 'I loved war too much,' and the dying monarch counseled the lad not to imitate this penchant. But this seems advice that the Sun King could never have taken himself. The dictates of *gloire* would never have allowed him a pacific course.

Further reading

Baxter, S., *William III and the Defense of European Liberty, 1650–1702*, New York, 1966.

Bromley, J. S., *Corsairs and Navies, 1660–1760*, London, 1987.

Chandler, D., *The Art of Warfare in the Age of Marlborough*, New York, 1976.

Chandler, D., *Marlborough as a Military Commander*, 2nd edn, London, 1979.

Childs, J., *The Army of Charles II*, London, 1976.

Childs, J., *The Nine Years' War and the British Army 1688–1697: The Operations in the Low Countries*, Manchester, 1991.

Churchill, W., *Marlborough, His Life and Times*, 4 vols, London, 1933–38.

Duffy, C., *The Fortress in the Age of Vauban and Frederick the Great, 1660–1789*, vol. 2: Siege Warfare, London, 1985.

Ekberg, C. J., *The Failure of Louis XIV's Dutch War*, Chapel Hill, NC, 1979.

Glete, J., *Navies and Nations: Warships and State Building in Europe and America, 1500–1860*, 2 vols, Stockholm, 1993.

Lossky, A., *Louis XIV and the French Monarchy*, New Brunswick, NJ, 1994.

Lynn, J. A., *Giant of the Grand Siècle: The French Army, 1610–1715*, New York, 1997.

Lynn, J. A., *The Wars of Louis XIV*, London, 1999.

McKay, D., *Prince Eugene of Savoy*, London, 1977.

Nosworthy, B., *The Anatomy of Victory: Battle Tactics, 1689–1763*, New York, 1990.

Parker, G., *The Military Revolution: Military Innovation and the Rise of the West, 1500–1800*, 2nd edn, Cambridge, 1996.

Scouller, R. E., *The Armies of Queen Anne*, Oxford, 1966.

Sonnino, P., *Louis XIV and the Origins of the Dutch War*, Cambridge, 1988.

Tallett, F., *War and Society in Early Modern Europe*, London, 1992.

Wolf, J. B., *Louis XIV*, New York, 1968.

Index

Related titles from Osprey Publishing

To order any of these titles, or for more information on Osprey Publishing, contact:

Osprey Direct (UK) *Tel:* +44 (0)1933 443863 *Fax:* +44 (0)1933 443849 *E-mail:* info@ospreydirect.co.uk

Osprey Direct (USA) c/o MBI Publishing *Toll-free:* 1 800 826 6600 *Phone:* 1 715 294 3345

Fax: 1 715 294 4448 *E-mail:* info@ospreydirectusa.com

www.ospreypublishing.com

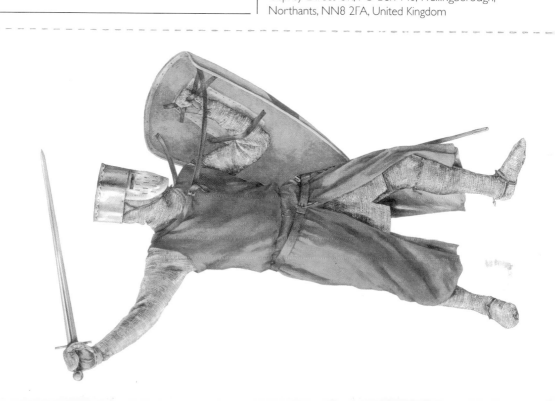

FIND OUT MORE ABOUT OSPREY

- ❏ Please send me a FREE trial issue of Osprey Military Journal
- ❏ Please send me the latest listing of Osprey's publications
- ❏ I would like to subscribe to Osprey's e-mail newsletter

Title/rank _____

Name _____

Address _____

_____

_____

_____

Postcode/zip _____

State/country _____

E-mail _____

Which book did this card come from?

_____

- ❏ I am interested in military history

My preferred period of military history is _____

- ❏ I am interested in military aviation

My preferred period of military aviation is _____

I am interested in (please tick all that apply)

- ❏ general history
- ❏ militaria
- ❏ model making
- ❏ wargaming
- ❏ re-enactment

Please send to:

USA & Canada:
Osprey Direct USA, c/o MBI Publishing,
PO Box 1, 729 Prospect Ave, Osceola, WI 54020, USA

UK, Europe and rest of world:
Osprey Direct UK, PO Box 140, Wellingborough,
Northants, NN8 2FA, United Kingdom

OSPREY
PUBLISHING

www.ospreypublishing.com

call our telephone hotline
for a free information pack

USA & Canada: 1-800-826-6600
UK, Europe and rest of world call:
+44 (0) 1933 443 863

Young Guardsman
Figure taken from *Warrior 22:
Imperial Guardsman 1799–1815*
Published by Osprey
Illustrated by Christa Hook

Knight, c.1190
Figure taken from *Warrior 1: Norman Knight 950 – 1204AD*
Published by Osprey
Illustrated by Christa Hook

POSTCARD